MVFOL

WINDOWS
MOVIE MAKER 2
ZERO TO HERO

Jon Bounds
John Buechler
Jen deHaan

friendsof

an Apress® company

WINDOWS MOVIE MAKER 2: ZERO TO HERO

ISBN (pbk):1-59059-149-6

Printed and bound in the United States of America 12345678910

Trademarked names may appear in this book. Rather than use a trademark symbol with every occurrence of a trademarked name, we use the names only in an editorial fashion and to the benefit of the trademark owner, with no intention of infringement of the trademark.

Distributed to the book trade in the United States by Springer-Verlag New York, Inc., 175 Fifth Avenue, New York, NY, 10010 and outside the United States by Springer-Verlag GmbH & Co. KG, Tiergartenstr. 17, 69112 Heidelberg, Germany.

In the United States: phone 1-800-SPRINGER, email orders@springer-ny.com, or visit http://www.springer-ny.com. Outside the United States: fax +49 6221 345229, email orders@springer.de, or visit http://www.springer.de.

For information on translations, please contact Apress directly at 2560 Ninth Street, Suite 219, Berkeley, CA 94710. Phone 510-549-5930, fax 510-549-5939, email info@apress.com, or visit http://www.apress.com.

Credits

Authors
Jon Bounds
John Buechler
Jen deHaan

Managing Editor
Sonia Mullineux

Technical Reviewer
Ben Forman

Indexer
Jo Crichton

Cover Design
Katy Freer

Copy Editor
Kristen Imler

Commissioning Editor
Jon Bounds

Editor
Adam Juniper

Project Manager
Jenni Harvey

Graphic Editor
Ty Bhogal

Author Agent
Gaynor Riopedre

Proof Reader
Jenni Harvey

At friends of ED, our mission is to unleash your digital creativity, providing technical know-how and inspiration in equal measure.

With our Zero to Hero series we've gone one better—we'll take you further, faster.

Zero to Hero is more than just a catchy slogan and an endless opportunity for gimmicks, puns, and graphical representations of phone booths, tights, and capes. It's a style of learning designed by friends of ED to reach beyond dry technical explanations and dusty old authors who wouldn't know good design if it slapped them round the face with a wet fish.

You can either first learn everything you need about Windows Movie Maker 2 or dive straight into the inspirational "Hero" chapters and refer back if you get stuck.

The authors of the Hero chapters are Movie Maker trailblazers from the friends of ED pool of talent. Each has a different brief and a lot of freedom. They'll show how you can achieve professional results with this remarkable program—how you too can be a Movie Maker 2 Hero.

And when you're done, you'll be ready to wear your underwear outside of your pants, metaphorically speaking of course.

We'll not only unlock the toolset for you, we'll also feed your imagination—that's a promise.

So, what are you waiting for?

About the authors

Jon Bounds is a writer and editor from Birmingham, England, where he grew up listening to the Smiths and trying to get his Sinclair Spectrum to do desktop publishing. Understandably, he was a morose child.

Jon studied for a Computer Science degree in the days when the Internet was still dismissed as a niche research tool, and digital video would never replace film. Despite these setbacks, he left the University of Birmingham with plans to use computers to create and share "stuff." A short-lived journalism career ended when he realized that he'd rather just make it all up—the *National Enquirer* had no vacancies.

He eschewed a crack at the big time as a Vegas lounge-singer because he couldn't face the possibility of a Copa Lounge engagement clashing with a Birmingham City F.C. match. Jon instead settled for the equally glamorous life of a Technical Editor at friends of ED. Now that computers have caught up a little, Jon spends many an hour editing video and isn't bored yet.

Keep Right On

John Buechler has been a photographer and videographer from the predigital days of film cameras and projectors to the nonlinear computerized editing of today. He uses many different photo and video editing software tools and, since its first release, he has been an avid user of Microsoft's Movie Maker.

He lives in Kalamazoo, Michigan. In addition to doing freelance video work, he applies his photography, video, and computer skills to home and family uses. He is called "Papa" by his grandchildren and is known by many on the internet as "PapaJohn." His personal web site http://pws.chartermi.net/, papajohn includes links to some of his movies.

PapaJohn is active on several Microsoft-sponsored multimedia newsgroups. You see him most often on microsoft.public.windowsxp.moviemaker, a key newsgroup for users of Movie Maker 2.

John was recognized by Microsoft as one of their 2003 Most Valuable Professionals in the Multimedia area. He recently expanded his support role by becoming a moderator of the Movie Maker 2 Special Interest Group (SIG) for the Windows Media Los Angeles Users Group at www.windowsmedia.org.

Jen deHaan is a freelance web designer/developer based in Calgary. She has been involved in writing, contributing to, or editing many computer books on Flash, ActionScript, digital video, and ColdFusion in 2002. She has co-authored three books on ActionScript for friends of ED: *Flash MX Designer's ActionScript Reference*, *ActionScript Zero to Hero*, and *Flash MX Most Wanted Components*. She was also a co-author of the *ColdFusion Developer's Handbook* published by Sybex and the forthcoming *Dreamweaver MX: ColdFusion Web Development*. Jen was a contributor and technical editor for six books published by Wiley and has several new titles in the works for 2003.

Jen graduated with top honors from a top New Media program and also with a BFA in Developmental Art from the University of Calgary. She is an experienced teacher and writer, focusing on integrating technologies for the web using Flash MX. Her personal web sites are www.ejepo.com and www.flash-mx.com.

Chapter Zero   1

Learn all the basics about digital video editing and get started by making a music video.

Chapter Zero

Shooting your footage   19

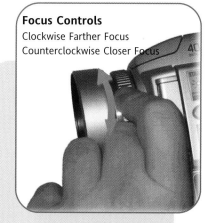

Focus Controls
Clockwise Farther Focus
Counterclockwise Closer Focus

Learn camera operation tips to improve the footage you shoot.

Chapter One

Capturing video and importing files 29

Capture your video from both analog and digital video cameras.

Chapter Two

Collections and projects 43

Organize your clips and start creating your movie projects.

Chapter Three

Transitions 73

Add professional-looking transitions between video clips and still images.

Chapter Four

Editing clips 87

Manipulate your footage at clip-level for fine control of your movie.

Chapter Five

Video effects 101

Add video effects to your movie and marvel at the results.

Chapter Six

Audio editing   115

Edit the soundtrack of your movie to add music and narration or to correct mistakes.

Chapter Seven

Titles and credits 137

Ms. Julia Gilbert
Canal Expert

Add captions, animated titles, and credits. Any size, font, or color.

Chapter Eight

Saving and sharing movies   147

Share movies by sending them
by e-mail, putting them on the
web, or making a CD, videotape,
VCD, or even DVD copy.

Chapter Nine

E-mailing a video postcard   177

Shoot, edit, and send video greetings by e-mail.

Hero 1

Editing a vacation movie   193

Capture your vacation memories forever in a professional-looking video with narration.

Hero 2

Videotaping an event   213

Produce a CD or DVD movie
centered on an event you attend.

Hero 3

Producing a short movie for the web   235

Produce a short film from script to final cut—and upload it to the Internet.

Hero 4

Chapter Zero

Whatever you want to make movies about—from your holidays to the fall of the Roman Empire—you've picked up this book for the same reason: you want to get the best out of Windows Movie Maker 2.

Learning a new piece of software can be a daunting task, especially one in a new area like video editing, and it's easy to get overwhelmed. Getting help can be fraught with tension: you don't want to look a fool, so you're frightened of asking the "easy" questions.

But it's only easy if you know the answer. You're no dummy or idiot; you just don't know anything about Movie Maker. However, just because your computer may baffle and irritate you at times and leave you feeling like a "zero," there's no need to worry—we can help with that. And we promise not to patronize you, either.

In this book, we'll show you all you need to know to make the movies you want with Movie Maker, as clearly and simply as humanly possible. That means letting you find the information you want quickly, not burying it deep within a story about problems we had house-training the dog. And we'll get down to business straight away.

This chapter looks at some basics, about digital video editing and Movie Maker itself, that you'll need under your belt (be that a superhero utility belt or something nice from Gucci) to get to grips with the rest of the book. If you're new to digital video, then some of them might seem a bit difficult, but trust us, if we get to grips with this now, then the rest will be a breeze. Once you've read Chapter Zero, then you can dip in and out of the book as *you* need. If you want to make a silent film, why spend hours learning about editing sound?

The aim of this book is to make you into a Movie Maker hero. Without doubt, you'll be excited about the filmmaking possibilities. Just don't blame us when you end up directing an epic in your yard, wildly over-budget with Grandma in a toga, shouting, "I am Spartacus!"

How to use this book

You're obviously itching to get started quickly; that's why you've chosen this book. The filmmaking process only operates one way; you can't roll out the red carpet for the premiere before you've shot the footage, and the book follows that logic. Each chapter is devoted to one aspect of the digital video creation process, and they're organized like this:

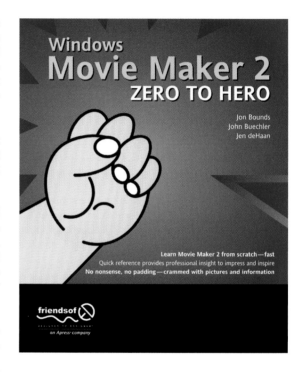

★ Chapter Zero, which you're already reading: This chapter covers all the basic concepts that you'll need under your belt to get the best out of Movie Maker.

★ Chapters One through Nine: We've arranged everything you'll want to make movies with Movie Maker into appropriate chapters. Although they're arranged in the order you'd complete one project, they're also broken into steps and examples that you can apply to your own work, dipping in wherever you choose.

★ Hero Chapters: It's all very well to be able to use the software, but sometimes it really helps to get inside the head of an experienced pro. We've added four chapters to get you thinking and working like the hero you undoubtedly are.

And all the way through, you'll find every step clearly illustrated so you can see exactly what's going on.

Styles

To make things even clearer, we've used separate typestyles throughout the book:

★ If we're mentioning an important technical term for the first time, we'll make it **bold**.

★ If we're directing you to something written on screen, it will appear on the page in a different font—this one.

★ Menu commands are written with arrows between the menu levels. For example, Clip > Video > Fade In would translate to what you see in the graphic to the right.

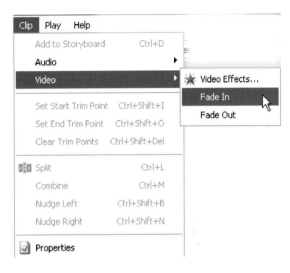

★ If we talk about using the keyboard, often indicating shortcut keys so that you can use Movie Maker faster, we'll write it like CTRL+C, meaning that you press the CONTROL key (abbreviated to CTRL on the keyboard, too) and the C key at the same time.

★ We'll also pick out web links that might be of interest, such as www.friendsofed.com.

★ If we have any specific files to mention, we'll write their filenames like MyVideo.WMV.

Finally, really important points and special tips will appear in boxes like, well, this one!

Download files

All the examples in the book are designed so that you can use the techniques with your own video footage—after all, you want to make movies with your friends and family in it, not someone else's.

There is never an instance in this book when you'll be unable to follow the instructions or understand the explanations without our video footage. However, if you need "movement" to make things clearer (this is a book about moving pictures, after all) you'll find extra examples to watch on our web site at www.friendsofed.com.

There you'll also find example movie footage to download, if you'd like to follow along with what we've done in specific exercises. It's organized in chapter-sized chunks, so you have to download only what you need.

Each of our Hero project movies is also available to watch and download in specially compressed web versions. Check them out and you'll see just what's possible with Movie Maker.

Support

We at friends of ED pride ourselves on our book support. Although we're confident that everything within these pages is easy to follow and error-free, don't hesitate to visit us at friendsofed.com or submit an email to support@apress.com.

Simply write to us, quoting the last four digits of the book's ISBN in the subject line (in this case, it's 1496), and even if our dedicated support team is unable to solve your problem immediately, your queries will be passed on to the people who put the book together.

And even if you don't have a problem, we'd love to hear from you. Requests for future books, queries about getting involved, or just telling us how much you love *Windows Movie Maker 2 Zero to Hero*—we're all ears.

If your question is about an issue not directly concerned with book content, then we've also got a number of message boards at friendsofed.com in the forums section. Here you'll find readers of all levels, as well as editors and authors, talking about how they use software like Movie Maker. They're all there because they enjoy sharing their knowledge, and we're sure you'll enjoy it just as much.

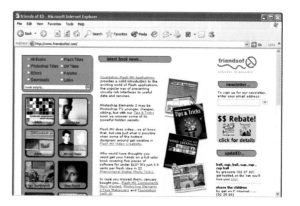

For software and Internet news and books on other aspects of the digital world with full details and sample chapters, downloads, author interviews, and more, just point your browser to www.friendsofed.com.

Types and sizes of video

Movie Maker can work with video captured from nearly all video cameras, even video recorders and TV tuners, which means that we need to understand a little about the way video is recorded and then stored on your computer.

Analog cameras and digital cameras

You can shoot your movie with any video camera, either analog, which records the footage as waves of information, or digital, which records footage as a series of 0s and 1s. The big advantage of digital formats is that they do not degrade (lose quality) as you copy them. With analog copies, each generation (a copy of a copy and so on) will have more noise and interference.

Video stored on digital videotape formats is easier to **capture** (transfer) onto a computer, because computers also store information in a digital format. Digital cameras were designed with this in mind, and so will have a DV-Out socket for connecting to a PC, as well as conventional video connections.

Video on analog tapes needs to be converted into digital format for it to be stored on a computer by a device known as a capture card.

NTSC and PAL

The video format of your camera will depend on where you live in the world (or where you bought your camera, at least). **NTSC** and **PAL** are the two main standards. The United States, Canada, and Japan use NTSC (National Television Standards Committee) format, and Europe and Australia use PAL (Phase Alternating Line).

The standards differ in the number of lines of dots they use to make up the picture. NTSC uses 525 lines from top to bottom on screen, and PAL uses 625. This is why you can't watch videos from the US on an English VCR, for example—it's not a conspiracy.

Computers don't care about NTSC and PAL formats anywhere near as much as TVs or VCRS; they don't have to receive or broadcast the pictures. This means that you have to tell Movie Maker which standard your video footage is in and capture and generate in the same format—otherwise, it will stretch or squash your video.

Another difference is that NTSC displays 30 frames per second, whereas PAL displays 25. If you capture video as NTSC and then record it back to videotape as PAL, it will slow down. If you capture as PAL and record back as NTSC, it will speed up.

Aspect ratio

The **aspect ratio** of video refers to the width and height of the picture and the relationship between them. Normal television screens have an aspect ratio of 4:3—for every four units (inches, centimeters, it doesn't matter) they are wide, they are three units high. Widescreen TVs have an aspect ratio of 16:9.

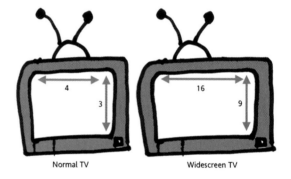

Normal TV   Widescreen TV

Many video cameras can shoot in both normal and widescreen modes, so it's important that you capture and generate your video with Movie Maker set to the right mode. If you capture video with Movie Maker set for 16:9 and then save your movie with Movie Maker set for 4:3, then the picture will be stretched to fit—it won't add black bars, as you might expect.

Nonlinear editing

In the old days, when you could leave your door open and the weather was better, films were edited by being cut up and then taped together again to produce the finished movie. It wasn't easy to test cuts before you decided whether they were the best ones, and it was a long, drawn-out process.

The process wasn't eased much by the invention of videotape. Banks of video recorders had to be wired together and clips had to be copied from the original tapes to the master, losing quality.

Nonlinear editing (NLE) is the real boon that has come from digital video. Just as word processors liberated people from the typewriter and correction fluid, NLE lets the user copy and paste video clips around like chunks of text. You can drag clips into new positions in your movies, remove them, and even put them back again as many times as you like until you're finally happy.

Nonlinear editing is also known as **nondestructive editing**, because the original video files that are captured are never destroyed or altered during the editing process. Instead, the computer maintains an **Edit Decision List (EDL)**, which stores references to the original video files on the hard drive and how they are arranged in a particular movie project.

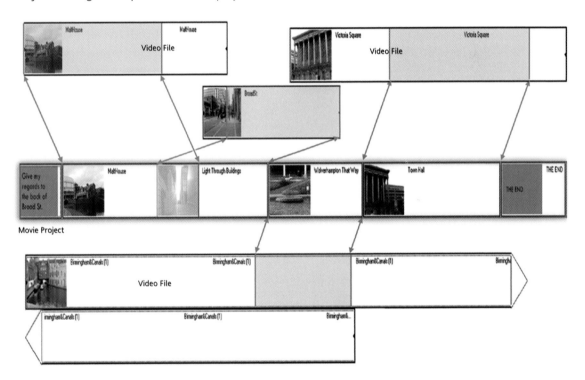

Creating an EDL is like hopping channels with the computer remembering what you watch—but being able to go back and change your mind if you didn't like it.

When you save your final movie file, the computer copies all the information it needs from the source files and **renders** a completely new video file.

Installing Movie Maker 2

If you haven't already got it, you can install version 2 of Movie Maker on your Windows XP computer by downloading it for free from the Microsoft web site. The download page is
http://www.microsoft.com/windowsxp/moviemaker/downloads/moviemaker2.asp.

The instructions are easy to follow, and you should have no problems with the installation. The first time you run version 2, it will automatically import any collections you had made with Movie Maker 1.

Movie Maker 2 Interface

When you open Movie Maker, it'll look something like this, although it may be arranged slightly differently if you've used it before, and there'll probably not be a pair of feet anywhere on screen. The main areas of the screen follow:

★ In the area at the far left, either the **tasks pane**, which offers a list of common things that you'll use Movie Maker to do, or the **collections pane**, which is a list of collections (folders) that you've created to organize your source materials.

★ The **collection contents** pane, where you select which video clips, pictures, or effects to use.

★ The **Preview Monitor**, where you can test exactly what your movie will look like when it's finished.

★ The **Storyboard/Timeline** window, where you build your movie clip by clip.

Tasks/Collections pane · Collection Contents pane · Preview Monitor

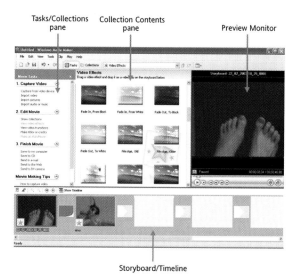

Storyboard/Timeline

Tasks pane

The Tasks pane lists a variety of common tasks that you can do with Movie Maker. They are organized under four headings:

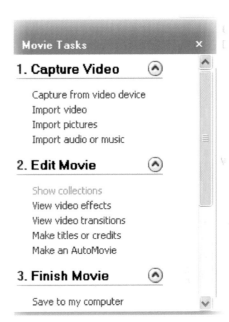

- ★ Capture Video—contains the different ways that you can get all your source materials into Movie Maker, not just video, but pictures and sound files, too.
- ★ Edit Movie—allows you to switch between clip collections and Movie Maker's effects and transition collections. It also offers the options to add titles and credits and to make an AutoMovie.
- ★ Finish Movie—lists the different ways that Movie Maker can save and generate your movie and lets you select them.
- ★ Movie Making Tips—is another way to access Movie Maker's help files, and are organized by task.

You can expand and collapse the headings by clicking on the arrows to their right.

Collections pane

In Movie Maker, you organize your source files (video clips, still images, and audio clips) within collections—just like folders in Windows. The collections pane lists these and shows these hierarchically.

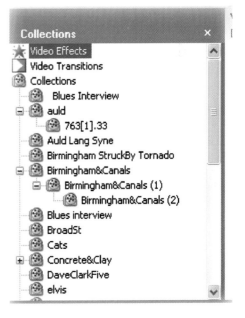

You can drag these folders into each other and create, delete, and rename them.

Select one, and whatever is in that collection appears in the collection contents pane.

At the top are Movie Maker's video effects and video transition collections.

Collection contents pane

The collection contents pane is where you select clips to put into your movies.

You can rename, delete, and drag clips in and out of the collections.

The collection contents pane acts very much like a folder window in Windows it allows you to choose between thumbnail view and a list and to order the clips by name, size, duration, and other properties.

Storyboard and timeline

The storyboard and timeline are one and the same; different ways of looking at how your movie is built. Changes made in one will be reflected in the other, and you can switch between them at any time by clicking on the Show Timeline or Show Storyboard buttons.

You build your movie by dragging clips from your collections into the storyboard/timeline, overlapping, trimming, and reordering them as you see fit.

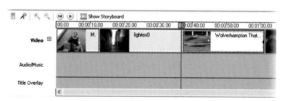

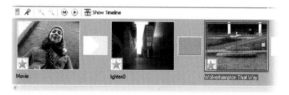

Preview Monitor

The preview monitor lets you see in detail what your finished movie will look like. If you select a clip (either in the collection contents pane or in the storyboard/timeline), then it is shown here.

The Preview Monitor also shows information about the clip (or the movie if you have selected the timeline), such as its length and name. You can play the clip here, controlling it with the buttons just as you would a video playing in your VCR.

Clicking on the Full Screen button will let you preview your clip or movie in the full space of your computer monitor.

Toolbar

The toolbar has five different sections.

Project tools   Undo/Redo   Tasks & Collections panes buttons   Collection tools   Collection details button

The first has familiar Windows buttons to start a new project, or to open or save one. Next are the Undo and Redo buttons.

Movie Maker remembers the last 10 things that you've done. Undo more than once to keep stepping back, or click on the arrow to the left of the button to open a list of choices to step back to.

If you've recently undone something, you can use the Redo button to step forward again in the same way.

The Tasks and Collections Panes buttons show or hide those panes.

The collection tools and the Collection Details button allow you to choose which collection you see in the collection contents pane and how its contents are represented.

Using the keyboard

Many functions in Movie Maker, both menu options and buttons, have a keyboard shortcut associated with them.

Some, like F1 for Help, will work no matter what you are doing in the program. Others will change their use depending on what you have selected in the timeline or collection contents pane.

If your keyboard settings are set to US, you can use the RETURN or ENTER key as well as the spacebar to play and pause the movie in the preview window.

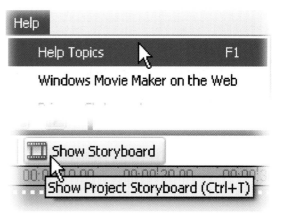

Customizing the interface

You can change the size of the different areas of the Movie Maker interface so that you can see more detail of the area you're concentrating on. Hover your mouse over one of the thick blue lines that divide one area from another, and the pointer will become a double-headed arrow.

Click and drag to alter the size of the different parts of the interface. Movie Maker has its limits, though, and won't allow you to fill the screen completely with one thing or another.

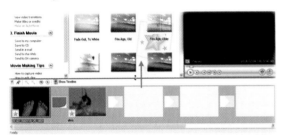 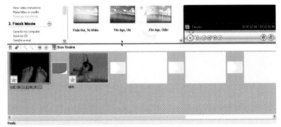

To open either the tasks or the collections panel, just click on the tasks, or Collections button in the toolbar to open one or the other. Or deselect them both to view neither, and have more room for the collection contents pane.

Preferences

The Options box, which you can open from Tools > Options, is where you set the preferences and defaults that will apply to all your Movie Maker projects.

On the General tab, you can enter a default author name, set the AutoRecover time and set Movie Maker to download automatically any **codecs** (compression software) it might need.

You can also set the Temporary storage directory. When it is rendering a movie to send back to your DV camera, via e-mail or to the web, Movie Maker has to keep a copy of the file on you computer until it has completed the job. These files can be large, so if you have more than one hard drive, you should set this to be the one with most space on it.

On the Advanced tab is where you set Movie Maker to capture and generate in NTSC or PAL and in the 4:3 or 16:9 aspect ratios.

File formats

Everything stored on your computer is one file type or another. Pictures are often stored as JPEGs, music as MP3s. Different file types organize the data in different ways, and not all programs can open each other's files—even if they deal with the same type of data. This can be because they have their own file formats and the programs are just not compatible, or because the programs have used different types of compression.

Compression

Most files on your computer are compressed. Compressing a file means that it will take less room on the hard drive or on a CD, and it will take less time to copy from one place to another, which is especially useful for transferring files across the Internet.

Just five frames of 525x425 video could be 3MB uncompressed.

Video files are in great need of compression. If you try to comprehend the amount of information that needs to be stored for just one fifth of a second of video, you'll soon realize why software giants are fighting to come up with the best video compression techniques.

If a video is running at 25 frames per second (as NTSC does) and is 525x425 pixels, then that is

(1/5 x 25) x (525 x 425) = 1,115,625 pixels

Each pixel could be up to 24 bits worth of information (depending on the color depth); that's 3MB of data in just one fifth of a second—without even considering the sound that goes with the video.

Compression comes in two broad types:

- ★ **Lossless**—finds patterns in the data and uses that information to squeeze it into a smaller space. A Zip file is an example of lossless compression.

- ★ **Lossy**—discards information that it calculates the human eye (or ear) won't notice is missing. This can be extra color information or sounds outside hearing range, as happens in an MP3.

Lossless compression is not all that useful for getting video files down to a manageable size; the detail in captured image files makes patterns unlikely.

One way that lossy compression compresses video while maintaining quality is by a process called statistical data redundancy. Look at these two frames from a piece of video. In the street scene, the traffic is at a standstill; there's no wind making the branches of the tree move. So the only thing that moves between the two pictures is the people. This means that the compression system can reduce file size by only keeping record of what changes from frame to frame.

When the traffic lights change and the buses move, there will be more data to change for each frame, but the buildings in the background will remain the same, allowing the file to still be smaller than it otherwise would have been.

Uncompressed 37.5MB for 9 seconds

The routines that decide which parts of the image data can be lost without seriously damaging the quality of the image are called **codecs** (compressor-decompressors). They remove the data from the file when compressing it and then use the same routine in reverse to fill in the gaps when the video is displayed.

> *To play a compressed video file, you need to have the same codec with which it was compressed.*

Compressed As WMV to 50KB

The programs that create and play WMV (Windows Media Video), like Movie Maker, can use new codecs by downloading them automatically from the Internet.

The more compressed a video is, the more noticeable the compression will be. You have to carefully judge file size against quality, depending on your priorities.

Importing

Movie Maker can import and use video, pictures, or audio files stored on your computer. Files with these extensions are accepted:

- ★ Video files: `.asf`, `.avi`, `.m1v`, `.mp2`, `.mp2v`, `.mpe`, `.mpeg`, `.mpg`, `.mpv2`, `.wm`, and `.wmv`
- ★ Picture files: `.bmp`, `.dib`, `.emf`, `.gif`, `.jfif`, `.jpe`, `.jpeg`, `.jpg`, `.png`, `.tif`, `.tiff`, and `.wmf`
- ★ Audio files: `.aif`, `.aifc`, `.aiff`, `.asf`, `.au`, `.mp2`, `.mp3`, `.mpa`, `.snd`, `.wav`, and `.wma`

> *Remember that anything you import has to already be on your computer's hard drive. If you want to use music from a CD in your movie, you have to copy the tracks onto your computer first into one of the accepted audio file types—Windows Media Player will easily do this for you.*

Exporting

Movie Maker creates only two types of files: WMV (Windows Media Video), which can be set to a wide variety of compression standards, and AVI (Audio-Video Interleaved) which is lossless.

Hard drive file systems

Hard drives set up to use the FAT32 file system don't allow files to be more than 4GB, even if there is enough room.

If you run into problems and it's not possible either to compress your movies or to make them shorter, you may need to add a hard drive that uses the NTFS file system or reformat your existing one. This is not a step to take lightly; ask an expert before attempting either of these options.

If you need to check what file system your hard drive uses, open Windows Explorer (press CTRL+E), right-click on your hard drive, and select Properties.

The file system is show in the disk properties box on the General tab.

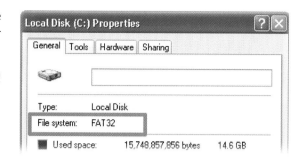

A word about copyright

Just because you've got copies of music, images, or video on your computer doesn't mean that you're allowed to use them to make your own movies.

You're unlikely to get sued for using a track from a CD on your own home movie, but once you distribute it more widely (yes, even one copy), you're on dangerous ground.

Check the copyright notice on anything you intend to use and distribute as part a movie, and ask the permission of the copyright holder.

The safest way is to compose your own soundtracks or use copyright-free material.

The first cut is the deepest

Phew, that was an awful lot of theoretical stuff and still not a whiff of your first Oscar nomination. As a little reward for getting though all that (it will come in handy, honest!), we're going to run though making a very simple movie—by using Movie Maker's much-lauded AutoMovie feature.

We're going to make a pop video for a garage band. You know the type, lots of ambition but not so much talent. If you'd like to follow this exactly, you can download the source video and music from www.friendsofed.com, but you can of course use any footage music (or any hapless band) you can find.

> If you're using your own files, you will need an audio file of at least 30 seconds and a video file of the same length or longer.

1. Open Movie Maker and start a new project (File > New Project or CTRL+N).

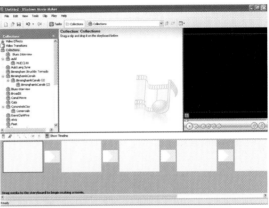

2. Go to the tasks pane and, from the Capture Video section, select Import Video.

3. A file browser will open. Navigate to the folder of download files for this chapter (or to that of your own video file).

4. Select the file TheInternationalClips or your own video file. Select the box that says Create clips for video files, and click on the Import button.

Movie Maker will create a new collection (calling it the same name as the video file) and import the file into it, breaking it into four clips. Movie Maker may produce more, or fewer, clips from another movie file.

5. Select Import pictures from the Capture Video section of the tasks pane. Navigate to the downloaded files on your computer and select the three JPG pictures. Click Import, and they will join your clips in the collection.

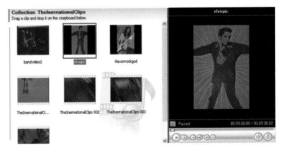

6. Choose Tools > AutoMovie…, and the AutoMovie wizard starts.

7. Select Music Video from the list of styles.

8. Click on Enter a title for the movie.

9. Type the name of the band, The International (or whatever your band is called), into the text box that appears.

10. Click on Select audio or background music.

11. Select Browse… and find the downloaded folder (or navigate to where your music file is kept). Select the MP3 file The International, and click Open.

12. Click on Done, edit movie. Movie Maker will now analyze the music and video files, looking for matching changes in tempo, and edit together a music video.

13. Press the Spacebar and watch the video in the preview monitor. It's not going to win an MTV award, but it's pretty good for a first effort.

Movie Maker tends to bunch still images together when it makes an AutoMovie, but then things won't be perfect if we let the computer make our decisions for us. The point is that, in just 13 easy steps, you got to watch a movie *you* had created, including a soundtrack and titles. Not bad going.

Naturally, you want more control over every aspect of your video, not least of all working your own footage, rather than letting these miscreants! So, now we've made our first rough cut; the rest of the book will set you on your way to heroic perfection.

Hoist up your tights. Hero status could be only days away!

Shooting your footage

In this chapter

In this chapter, we'll look at what you can do to improve your finished movies before you even turn on your computer, including simple ways you can maximize the quality of the video you shoot and enjoy yourself more in the process.

However experienced you become at digital video editing, or however much you spend on computer packages, there's still very little you can do to improve badly shot footage. If you think a little before and during your shoot, though, it's easy to capture some great video to work with.

We'll cover the following:
- ★ Basic camera operation
- ★ Keeping the camera steady
- ★ Lighting
- ★ Focus
- ★ Camera movement, zooming, and panning
- ★ Recording sound

Getting to know your camera

Most digital video cameras are quite simple to operate, but unless you familiarize yourself with the machine itself, its controls, and menus, you'll always end up being unprepared at a crucial moment—that's Murphy's Law!

How to read the manual

The instruction manual that came with your camcorder, no matter how badly written, will contain all the information you need to operate it. People are often fazed by the technical nature of the explanation, but there's no need to be.

There's nothing to be gained by reading the manual from cover to cover in one sitting. It's not a novel. The best way to read an instruction manual is to refer only to the information you need. When you need to learn about manual focus, for example, use the index and table of contents and only read what you need.

> *You'll learn more from experimenting with your camera than from its instruction manual. As long as you have the basics under your belt, the learning experience should be fun.*

Batteries and power

Your camera will probably have been supplied with a battery that fits in or on the machine somewhere and a power cord to connect it to an electrical outlet. It will also have somewhere on the box or in the manual a claim about how long the camera will last without needing to be recharged. Take these claims with a grain of salt; they are likely to be a maximum time, based on one completely charged, full battery.

If your camera has an LCD screen for viewing as you shoot, this will take up more power than watching through your viewfinder. If power is running low, it's best to switch to viewing through the eyepiece.

Spare batteries are a great idea, and you can often purchase ones that have a greater power capacity than those supplied with your camera as standard.

Ask at your local electrical store or check out the manufacturer's web site for details.

If you are filming from one position for a length of time and there's an electrical outlet nearby, you can always plug in your camera.

Tape length and formats

Be aware of the length of the video cassettes that you are using, especially if you are filming an event that lasts for a long time. Most tapes will last either for 60 or 90 minutes, although your camera may have a long play function.

If you're shooting a play with an intermission (or a soccer game), for example, it would be best to swap to a fresh tape for the second half. That way you know that there'll be enough room left.

There are many different formats of video cassette, so always check that you're buying the right kind. Taking a tape with you to the store when getting new ones can save a lot of hassle.

Controls while shooting

The basic functions of the camera that you'll use during filming are **zoom** and **focus**, two terms that you'll have heard before. These will be controlled in slightly different ways on each individual camera, but the zoom control will normally be a slider on the right side of the machine and the focus controlled by a wheel around the lens. Most cameras have an automatic focus feature, but there are times when you'll need to do it manually. For example, if you know that your subject and camera won't move, then manual focus will stop the automatic focus from hunting and ruining your shot.

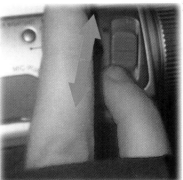

Zoom Controls

Up—Widen Angle

Down—Tighten Angle

You should practice with these controls before you attempt to film anything important, which you can do without recording. These, more than any others, are controls that will affect the look of the finished article.

Focus Controls

Clockwise
Farther Focus

Counterclockwise
Closer Focus

We'll learn more about zooming and focus later in the chapter, but take a look at the controls on your camera and familiarize yourself with their operation.

Keeping the camera steady

Nothing shows up home movies (or "amateur footage," as they always seem to call it on the news) as much as "camera wobble". Your audience will be used to seeing footage shot on professional equipment that's rock-solid—any movement will distract them. So unless you're filming your own *Blair Witch* sequel, anything you can do to minimize the shake is well worth doing.

Tripods

Tripods are worth investigating and investing in if you intend to do a lot of "planned" shooting. They are invaluable if you are using your camera at weddings or other events where the focus of the action doesn't change. Along with the benefit of steady footage, they also allow you to leave the camera to its own devices and get more involved with the party!

Holding the camera

Tripods are not always practical. They are heavy and awkward to carry, and in many cases, you won't have time to set them up in each location you'd like to film. You can still do a lot to keep the camera steady by thinking about the way that you hold it in your hands.

Camcorders are getting smaller and lighter all the time, and any movement of your arm will be multiplied when you come to see the footage. Steady your camera arm with your other hand by holding your bicep, which will restrict its vertical movement.

If it's practical, steady your whole body by leaning against a wall. Plant your feet firmly and rest your body against the surface of the wall.

Filming this way will make accidental movement difficult, and any camera move will have to be deliberate. You won't move, unless the wall does.

If you're filming something nearer to the ground than you are, don't be afraid to kneel. Getting down to the level of the children, for example, will improve the shots greatly. Holding the camera in two hands with an elbow on your knee will steady the camera perfectly.

If you're using the camera's LCD screen to watch as you film, use two hands to hold and steady the camera. Cradle the camera underneath and tilt the screen to enable you to view it without stooping—this'll help you to look away and back to the camera without jogging it or moving it unexpectedly.

Keeping steady on the move

You may have seen professional camerapeople use a device called a Steadicam. They are used most often in films, when the camera follows an actor as he or she walks through a scene. You may also have seen them on sports report shows when a coach is being interviewed on the pitch following the game.

They work by giving the camera a lower center of gravity. That complex-looking machinery is really just a weight connected to the bottom of the camera. Though we don't need to get into the science of this right now, we can use the principle to help us.

If you have a tripod, you can leave it connected to the bottom of your camera with the legs folded in.

If not, and you don't mind looking a little silly, you can attach your own weight by using a piece of string. Here we used a sock with a pool ball in it, but you can use anything you like. A small object, weighing around two pounds is most suitable, and it really will improve your movies.

Lighting

It's important to think about both the amount of light that you camera has and where it is coming from. You can't always control the lighting as much as you'd like (the sun, for example, is always going to be out of your hands!), but knowing a little about how light affects your camera can improve things tremendously.

Outside lighting—the sun

Filming directly into the sun is a bad idea, generally. Although it can create some nice effects, it will make sections of your image appear extremely dark—as you can see, it is difficult to make out any detail toward the front of this shot.

If possible, stand with your back to the sun, allowing it to light your scene evenly.

Interior lighting

You have more control of how your scenes are lit when you are indoors, but there are still issues to be aware of.

If your subject is too near to the strongest, or only, light source, it will appear almost completely in shadow. Altering the angle you shoot from, even by a little will make everything clearer. Again, shooting away from the light source produces much clearer footage.

As a general rule, whatever you shoot will look darker than it did in real life—so always make sure that you make the most of whatever light there is.

If you'd like to see this in action, you can watch Window Light Example at the downloads section on www.friendsofED.com.

Night shooting

Some camcorders will be equipped with a Night Shot function, which digitally brightens the video as you shoot it. You may have seen this effect on nature documentaries.

Focus

Focusing can be a tricky subject. Although autofocus cameras have made it seem to be less important, there are a few things that you still need to be aware of.

Autofocus

As good as autofocus mechanisms have become over the years, there's no way that the camera can know what is the most important object in your shot. Autofocus simply guesses based on size and position, so it can get it wrong.

The building in the distance cannot be seen using autofocus. You can see this example, Night Focus at the downloads section on www.friendsofED.com.

Bright light sources in otherwise subdued light particularly cause problems. In these cases, even with the most expensive camcorders, you will have to go back to the old-fashioned method.

Autofocus will also take a second or two to right itself after a speedy camera move, which isn't a fault but rather something to be aware of.

Manual focus

If you decide to use manual focus, you will have to first switch off the autofocus function on your video camera and then rotate the focus wheel to bring the focus onto your chosen object.

With focus set to 0.1m, the doll in the foreground is blurred, but as the wheel is turned counterclockwise, the doll in the background is brought into focus. Most cameras show the focal length (the distance that an object would need to be away to be in focus) when you alter it.

You can watch the focus happen in Focus Example at www.friendsofED.

Focus-pulling

It's rare to see focusing in a finished movie, as it reminds the viewer that they are watching a film. It can be used to bring attention to a smaller object in the picture or transfer attention from one person to another—this is know as **focus-pulling**.

Camera moves

Camera moves are the movements that the camera seems to make when you are watching the final movie, which doesn't necessarily mean that the camera itself moved while you were filming. Zooming and panning are the two that you are most likely to come across.

Zooming

A camera zoom is when the camera appears to move closer (**zooming in**) or further away (**zooming out**).

In reality the camera stays in a fixed position and a second lens within the camera moves, altering the magnification of the camera's view. This is called an **optical zoom**. Most digital video cameras also have a **digital zoom** function, which will allow you to continue to zoom in further than the lens can move.

> *Digital zoom leaves the lenses alone and simply looks at a smaller and smaller area of the scene. The camera then guesses at (interpolates) the information that's missing.*

You can normally hear when digital zoom kicks in as the whirring of the lens mechanism stops. To ensure that your picture stays at maximum quality, you should be able to turn off the digital zoom or avoid using it.

Zooming speed

Some cameras allow you to control the speed of a zoom by how far you push the zoom control one way or the other, or in the menu options. The faster a zoom is, the more noticeable it will be to your audience, whereas one that varies in speed will seem jerky and will almost always spoil the effect.

If you're going to zoom, you should do it as smoothly as possible.

Zoom sparingly

Because you want your audience to concentrate on *what* you're filming rather than on the film itself, it's best to avoid zooms altogether in your finished movie.

> *When you come to edit your final movie, you can cut (remove) the part of the film that shows the zoom and jump from one point to another. Your movie will look all the more professional for it.*

When you're zoomed in, beware that any movement you make will be multiplied on screen. The slightest knock will make the camera shake uncontrollably. If you know that you are going to be zoomed-in on an object for a long time, it may be better to move closer to it (especially if your only other option is digital zoom).

If you would like to see just how cutting out the zoom can improve your movie, check out Zooming Example at the downloads section on www.friendsofED.com.

Panning

A **pan** is when the camera's viewpoint moves from left to right, right to left, or up to down. Unlike zooming, you have to move the camera physically, although you yourself should remain as still as possible.

Pans are great for establishing a scene, giving the audience the background to where the action will take place.

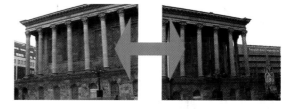

You can watch this example on Pan at the downloads section on www.friendsofED.com.

Panning speed

As with zooming, a fast or jerky pan will be noticed by your audience, so be careful to shoot pans at a relaxed pace. They are all about your audience absorbing the atmosphere of a place, so pan slowly and take in as much as possible.

Other camera movement

Most other onscreen movement is created by moving the camera itself. Moving toward or away from an object is known as a **truck** (because in the movies, that's how they're shot—with the camera on a little truck). It will happen naturally as you move; all you really need to do is keep the camera as steady as you can.

In-camera effects

Different video cameras have different effects available. Without going into detail about specific makes and models, there's one important thing to think about. If you apply an effect to footage as you shoot it, you can't remove it. With footage on your computer, however, you can experiment as much as you like—and return to the original if you decide to.

Recording sound

You have far less control over sound than any other section of your video. The microphones built into most camcorders are not directional, meaning that they record sound from all directions. This can be a problem. Remember that you are much closer to the camera than your subjects are—you may even be able to hear yourself breathing.

If the sound will be an important feature in your movie, it is worth considering connecting a microphone to your camera. **Clip-mics** (or tie-mics, as they're also known) are a perfect solution if you have a person talking directly to camera, in an interview situation, for example.

If your sound does turn out to be poor, don't worry too much because computer editing techniques can often improve or replace bad sound. Some carefully chosen background music can hide a multitude of sins.

Practice makes perfect

It may seem obvious, but you really will get better at shooting video the more you do it. So, if you've got a new video camera, it's not wise to make your first movie a friend's wedding—make your mistakes with footage that you don't have to show people.

Gain some confidence by capturing your pets or animals in your garden. Animals will act naturally in front of a camera, and that's useful when practicing because you don't have to worry about their reactions. Look—neither of these squirrels is worrying about how fat they look.

Capturing video and importing files

In this chapter

Whatever you have shot with your video camera, whatever pictures you've taken, whatever music or soundtracks you've decided to use—you've got to get them into your computer and get Movie Maker 2 to recognize them.

Movie Maker can capture video directly from your camera (assuming that you can connect it) whether it's digital or analog. It can also import many types of video files created with other software, as well as pictures taken with your digital camera and sound and music files, allowing you to mix and manipulate all of these into your own movies. Once captured or imported, all of these things remain available to you to use in as many projects as you would like. We'll go through the whole process in this chapter, as well as offer helpful advice if it doesn't go quite as planned for you. This chapter will cover

★ Connecting your camera to your PC
★ Video formats and types
★ Configuring an analog capture device
★ Capturing digital and analogue footage
★ Storing your captured video
★ Importing video, audio, and picture files
★ Taking still pictures from your video footage

Connecting your camera

All video cameras are different, and wildly differently priced, but broadly, they fall into two categories, **analog** and **digital**. They are connected to and work with your PC in different ways, but each needs the appropriate **port** (socket) and connecting cable. Sometimes the appropriate hardware will already be installed in your computer when you buy it—if not, you will have to add a piece of hardware with the port and capture circuits to it. Which type you need depends on your camera.

Digital cameras

Digital cameras are connected to computers by means of a system known as **FireWire** (officially called IEEE 1394 and, for reasons best known to themselves, called i.Link by Sony). This is a standard of data transfer, incredibly fast compared to other types of connections, that allows data to be transferred along it in either direction. This means that as well as receiving information, your computer can send information to your digital camera (and even control it).

If you have a newer PC, you may already have a FireWire port on your computer. If not you can add one as long as you have a free PCI slot. These (also know as expansion slots) allow you to plug in extra hardware—which, in the case of a FireWire card, Windows should recognize and install automatically.

These cards are simple to install and not expensive, so even the inexperienced should be able to add them by following the instructions supplied. Of course, if you are nervous, you should allow an expert to fit any extra hardware needed.

Computer

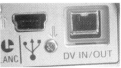

Firewire Ports   Camera

When you're all FireWire equipped, you are ready to connect your camera with the FireWire cable. You'll connect this from the port on your computer to your camera's DV-Out socket. Your camera may also have other connections (USB, A/V Out, etc.), but it's only the DV-In/Out sockets that are used with FireWire transfer. Simply plug the cable into the appropriate ports on your computer and video camera.

If you switch your camera on when it's connected to your computer, Windows will recognize it and open the Digital Video Device window. You'll be given a list of programs installed on your computer that can work with a digital camera and be asked if you want to launch one of them. You can use this window to open Movie Maker if you don't already have it running.

Analog cameras

To connect an analog video device (which can include a VCR or a TV tuner) to your PC, you will need a **capture device**. These not only provide a port with which to connect a video device but also contain chips which convert the analog signal it supplies into digital information that your computer can store.

If you want to use video that has been recorded onto analog videotape, then these are the main options. They can be fitted to a PCI slot or a USB port and accept input in different ways—most usually S-Video and standard Composite video formats—so you will have to check that your video camera (or VCR) has the appropriate output. Pinnacle Systems (www.pinnaclesys.com) are a major manufacturer and supplier of capture cards while Belkin (www.belkin.com) offer a number of solutions that won't require you to open your PC.

Most analog connections are one-way, which will mean that you can't record your Movie Maker productions back onto videotape with them. With analog cameras and video players, you will also have to control playback yourself; your computer can't control them directly.

Capturing analog video with a DV camera

Some digital video cameras allow you to connect an analog source to them, often through the A/V In socket, and this is another option for capturing analog video for use with Movie Maker. Sometimes you will need to record the analog footage onto a DV tape first and then capture as you would digitally recorded video, but some DV cameras allow you to use a pass-through capability. If you are using pass-through, you can capture the analog footage as if you were recording live video from your DV camera. This can be a complex issue and is different with each model of camera—www.dvdrhelp.com/capture is a great source of tips and advice.

Sony markets a number of Digital 8 cameras, which record digitally onto tapes the same size as analog 8mm or Hi8 videotapes. They will also play (and allow capture from) the analog formats, making them really handy if you've got 8mm/Hi8 tapes lying around.

Compatibility

Not all cameras or capture devices will be compatible with Windows XP or Movie Maker (check with their manufacturer if you're not sure). In this case, you will have to use the software supplied with them to capture your video footage and then import it into Movie Maker.

Sony MicroMV cameras, for example, use an MPEG format that cannot be directly captured by Movie Maker. You have to use the supplied MovieShaker software to get the video onto your computer.

Dazzle Video capture systems (both the 100 and 150 models) can only be used with their Movie Star 5 software—although you can save AVI files and import them into Movie Maker.

Setting video properties

Before you start to capture, check your video properties. Open the Options dialog box (Tools > Options) and click on the Advanced tab.

You should make sure that your Video format: and Aspect ratio: options are set the same as the video that you are about to capture.

Select NTSC or PAL depending on what format your camera records in (NTSC for the US, PAL for Europe). Aspect ratio (the ratio of width to height of the video image) can be switched between 4:3, which is the normal TV style, or 16:9, which is widescreen.

Starting the Video Capture wizard

With Movie Maker open and your camera connected and switched on, there are two ways that you can start the Video Capture wizard, and hence the capture process.

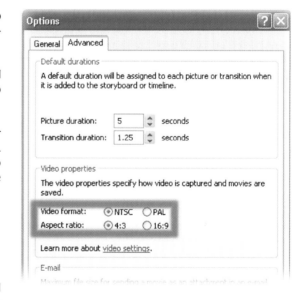

Select Capture from video device from the task pane, or select File > Capture Video... (CTRL+R).

If you haven't connected your video camera correctly or it isn't switched on into a mode that Movie Maker can work with, you will see this warning box. Check all connections and settings, then try again.

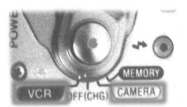

For capturing video from DV tape, the camera will have to be in the VTR or VCR position.

For capturing live direct from the camera's lens, the switch will have to be in the Camera position. If your DV camera supports pass-through and you're using this feature to capture analog footage, you should also use this position.

Selecting the video device

If you have more than one video device connected and powered up when you start the wizard, you will be allowed to select which one you would like to capture from. This page of the Video Capture wizard will not appear if you only have one digital camera connected to the computer; you will be sent straight to the next page.

If you select an analog capture device, you will be allowed to adjust a number of input settings, including the following:

★ Video input source—Lists the available sources, if an analog capture device has multiple input connections. You need to choose which source to use for capturing video. If only one source is available, you will not see this option.

★ Audio device—Lists the available audio capture devices you can use for capturing audio. If you only have one audio capture device, that device is selected automatically.

★ Audio input source—Lists the available audio sources, assuming your capture device has more than one input. You should choose the appropriate one for your video source.

★ Input level—Shows and allows you to adjust the volume of captured audio. The display is very much like that of a graphic equalizer on a stereo system, the bar rising and falling with the volume levels. You will need to start your source playing in order to test the audio levels.

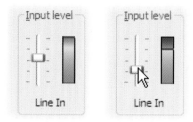

If the Input level is set too high, with the bar often in the red portion of the display, sound will be muffled and distorted. If it is set too low, you won't be able to hear it properly. Drag the slider down with your mouse until the levels show mostly in the green portion, only occasionally peaking into the red.

Configuring an analog capture device

If you click on the Configure button, a dialog box will open, in which you can alter the capture settings of your particular device. Exactly what options will be available and what the box will look like will depend on the drivers used for your device. If your video capture device uses Windows Driver Models (WDM) drivers, the Configure Video Capture Device box will be used. If your capture device uses Video for Windows (VFW) software drivers, it will open its own customized box.

> *You will have to check the manual that came with your video capture device for specific information about which settings you will have control over.*

★ **Camera Settings**—Control settings such as color, brightness, and contrast of the captured video.

★ **Video Settings**—Settings such as the display size and compression settings for your captured video fall into this category.

★ **TV Tuner**—If your device has a TV tuner, you will be able to change the channel and the video format.

When you've selected and configured your video device, click on Next and you'll be taken to the next page of the Capture Video Wizard.

Storing captured video

As you capture video footage onto your PC, it will be converted to a computer video file and saved onto a hard disk. The file can then be used in Movie Maker; you'll copy, split, and alter pieces of it to create your movie, but this will never change the file itself. The file that you capture is never changed or destroyed by Movie Maker—instead, it stores a list of references to your edits and will create your final movies as separate, self-contained files.

Choosing where to store captured video

The wizard asks you what you would like to call the captured video file and where you would like it to be saved.

1. Enter a file name for your captured video—You can name your file anything you like, within normal Windows conventions. Choose a name that will allow you to identify the file later.

2. Choose a place to store your captured video—You can pick a folder from the drop-down menu, which will offer you frequently used folders. You can also click on Browse... and choose any folder on your hard disks, even create a new folder and name it, if you wish.

Video files are large and need to be accessed as quickly as possible for best quality playback. If you have more than one hard drive, you should pick the one with most space left on it.

In any case, it's wise to defragment your hard disk regularly (go to All Programs > Accessories > System Tools > Disk Defragmenter from the Start menu). This ensures that files are stored all in one block on the disk, instead of in bits and pieces wherever the computer finds space. You should do this every time before you start a new capture session, especially if your hard disks are quite full.

3. Click on Next when you've selected where to save your video file.

Selecting a video setting

The Video Setting page of the wizard is where you can control the compression and quality of the video that you're about to capture.

If you're using a FireWire-connected DV camera, you'll have the pick of all the options here, but if you're using an analog capture device, only the ones that it can supply will be shown.

The Setting details part of the page will show you the quality of a video file captured with the selected settings.

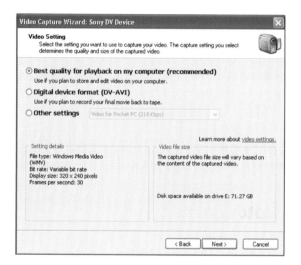

★ The File type will either be WMV, which can be played on computers with Windows Media Player installed, or AVI, which is an uncompressed video file format that produces large files of the best-quality possible.

★ The Bit rate of a video file refers to the number of bits (pieces of digital information, a 1 or a 0) that need to be processed by the program playing back the file. Even compressed video contains thousands of bits in each frame, so this figure is normally expressed in kbps (number of kilobits per second, 1kb = 1024b) or Mbps (Megabits per second, 1Mb = 1000kb).

★ The Display size is the size in pixels of the video image, and Frames per second is the number of complete images that the computer will store for every second of video.

The Video file size section will show the space available for capture on your selected drive and also the file size of video captured at this setting.

The Best quality... setting will produce a WMV file that will look good on your computer. This is the setting to choose if you are only going to use this footage to make movies to be shown on a computer.

The Digital device format setting will produce an AVI file of your captured video. AVI files are not compressed and so produce the best possible reproduction of digital video. Analog capture devices may not have this setting. If you want to transfer movies made with this footage back to videotape, or make a VCD or DVD, you should choose this setting.

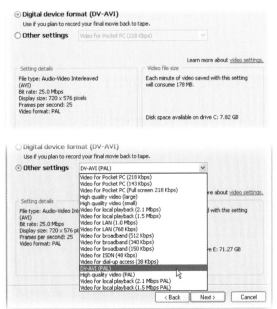

The Other settings, selectable from the drop-down box, will produce WMV files of different sizes and qualities. They are listed by types of playback, and the Video settings (bit rate, display size, and frames per second) are optimized for each kind of playback. This is useful if you are intending to make a movie for Internet playback only, for example, and this will let you work with a video that looks exactly like the finished version will.

You should select the quality required for your output and then click Next.

Capturing video

If you have a digital camera, you can capture video automatically, allowing Movie Maker to capture the entire tape. If you prefer, you can manually capture only parts of the videotape. Choose one and click on Next.

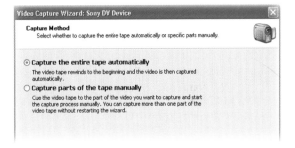

Analog capture devices can only be captured manually, and if you are using one, you will not see this page of the wizard.

Automatic capture

The DV capture when capturing automatically is almost fully automated; you just watch as Movie Maker does all the hard work.

It first rewinds your videotape to the start and then starts playing it, capturing the video to a file as it goes.

It shows the length of the captured video in hours, minutes, and seconds and also the size of file that will be created in KB. You are also shown the amount of disk space available for capturing onto (in GB).

If you decide to stop the capture (in that you think all the video you need is already captured), click on the Stop Capture button, and you will see this warning:

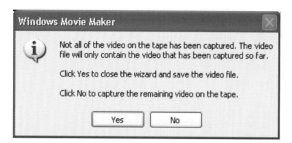

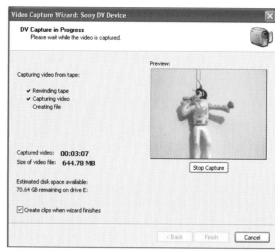

When you've finished capturing, choose whether or not to let Movie Maker create clips, and click Finish. (What Movie Maker does when it creates clips is discussed under the heading "Importing the files to your collections" later in the chapter.)

Manual capture

Once you've selected the capture format and quality, you're presented with the same Capture Video box for analog or digital capture.

It shows you a preview of the video source as well as the length of the captured video in hours, minutes, and seconds and the size of file that will be created in KB.

You are also shown the amount of disk space available for capturing onto (in GB).

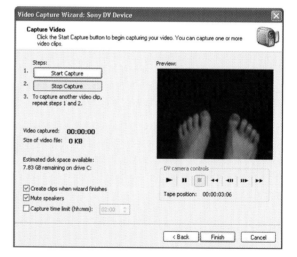

If you are using a DV camera, you can use the icons in the DV camera controls section to cue your videotape to the start of the parts that you want to capture. They act in the same way as the controls on the camera itself, although there may be a slight time delay in the operation being performed by the camera.

Digital videotapes with a timecode also show the position in the tape.

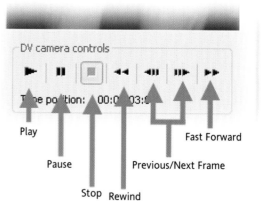

By using these controls, especially the Previous and Next Frame buttons, you have extremely accurate control over which parts of the tape to capture.

Your computer can't control analog devices, so you won't have these controls on the Capture Video page. You need to use the controls on your camera or VCR to cue the tape.

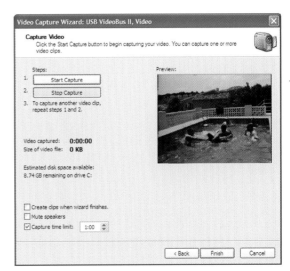

If you're recording live, either direct from the camera or by using pass-through to record from another source, then these controls will also be absent.

The capture process is the same whatever device you're using:

1. Cue the video source to the point at which you'd like to start capturing. Pause the tape.

2. Click the Start Capture button. If you're using the DV controls, then Movie Maker will automatically start running the tape. If not, then you will have to start the video device manually—do this after selecting Start Capture so you don't miss anything.

3. Watch as your video is captured, then when you've captured enough of this portion of the video, click on Stop Capture.

4. You can then cue your tape to another point and click Start Capture as many times as you like, capturing footage from different parts of the same tape (or even different tapes) within one file.

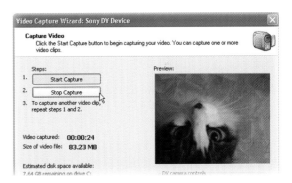

If you use the DV controls on the Preview window (or the controls on your digital camera itself) while you're capturing video, then Movie Maker will automatically stop capturing.

If you know the exact length of a piece of video that you'd like to capture, you can set a Capture time limit (in hours and minutes). Select the box and set the time limit by clicking on the hours or minutes figure and using the up and down arrows.

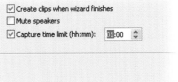

If you would like to turn off the computer speakers and listen to the audio from your camera, select the Mute speakers box.

When you've finished capturing, choose whether or not to let Movie Maker create clips, and click Finish.

Importing the files to your collections

When you click Finish in the Video Capture Wizard, the file created is saved to your hard drive—with the file name you gave it right back at the start of the process.

The file will then be imported into a Movie Maker collection of the same name as a clip. If you had Create clips… selected, then Movie Maker will try to identify "scenes" (based on big changes in the video) and split the video file into a number of different clips. This is useful if there really are distinct scenes in your captured file or it's really long and splitting it up will make it more manageable. For an in-depth look at clips within collections, see **Chapter 3**.

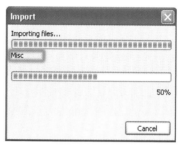

Importing files on your computer

Movie Maker can work with still pictures and audio and music files that are stored on your computer, as well as video files that you may have created with other programs. For Movie Maker to recognize them and for you to be able to use them in your movie projects, you have to import them into a collection.

1. Select the collection that you'd like to import the files to, or create a new one. For the full run down on creating collections, see **Chapter 3**. Video files will automatically have a new collection created for them.

2. Either select File > Import into Collections (CTRL+I) or select the type of file to import from the Tasks pane.

3. You'll see a standard Windows XP file browser and be able to navigate to the files that you want to import in the normal way.

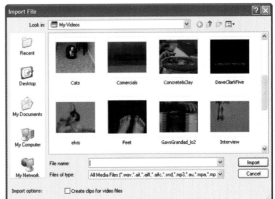

The Files of type: box will show either the acceptable video, picture, or audio file formats if you selected one from the Tasks pane or a list of all acceptable media file formats if you opened the browser from the menu. You can alter this if you want to import files of a specific type.

4. Select the file(s) that you'd like to import. You can select more that one file, if you want (consecutive files by using the SHIFT key or individually by using the CTRL key).

5. Click Import and your files will appear in the selected collection as thumbnails in the Collection contents pane.

Movie Maker can import most common types of picture and audio files. JPEGs (the most common type exported by digital still cameras) and MP3 files (the ubiquitous audio format) present no problems. For a full list of supported file types, see **Chapter 0**.

You can allow Movie Maker to create clips from imported video files in the same way as it does from captured video. If you want this, select the Create clips for video files box in the file browser.

Importing MOV files

The most problematic import is the MOV video file type. This is a format created by Apple's QuickTime software, and Movie Maker can't import it directly. If you have a video clip in MOV format, you will first need to convert it to a format that Movie Maker can accept (AVI is easiest). To do this you will need another piece of software.

QuickTime Pro (www.apple.com/QuickTime) can do this easily and is a useful tool to have if you're doing a lot of video work. Registration costs around $30.

If you don't envisage doing this often, RAD Video tools (www.radvideotools.com) has a free tool that will do MOV to AVI conversion, among other things.

> *Remember that Movie Maker creates only references to files, not copies of them. Files that you import have to be available at all times. Copy the files onto your hard drive, don't move or delete them.*

Taking a still from a video clip

If you would like to use a frame of a video clip as a still image in your movie (maybe for a "freeze-frame" effect), Movie Maker can capture and save a JPEG picture file from any video clip.

1. Select a video clip in Movie Maker, whether in the Collection contents pane or in the storyboard/timeline.

2. Play it in the Preview Monitor and pause it on the frame that you'd like to use.

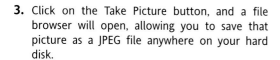

3. Click on the Take Picture button, and a file browser will open, allowing you to save that picture as a JPEG file anywhere on your hard disk.

When it's been saved, the picture will be imported into your current collection for you to use as you would any other still image.

The size of the picture depends on where the clip was selected. If you take a picture from a clip in the Collection contents pane, it will be the same as the original source video file. However, if you take a still picture of a frame of video from a clip on the storyboard/timeline, the picture will be 320x240 pixels.

Collections and projects

In this chapter

A project in Movie Maker 2 is where you produce a complete definition of your movie. You start with an empty storyboard or timeline and create the movie by adding video clips, still pictures, background music, narration, and text. You polish it off with special video effects and transitions between scenes. When you've completed your movie, Movie Maker uses the information in the project to create the movie.

Here we'll explore the things that go into a project, and how to control them to suit our movies. Most will be thoroughly covered while some, such as transitions and effects, will be briefly touched on as other chapters are wholly devoted to them.

We'll cover
- ★ Source footage and files
- ★ Creating and managing collections and their contents
- ★ Importing source files into collections as clips
- ★ Creating projects in Movie Maker
- ★ Editing with the storyboard and timeline
- ★ Using AutoMovie to create a project
- ★ How to add text, effects, and transitions
- ★ Saving and reviewing your project

A project is not a movie

When you work on a movie, you build up the movie as information in a **project** file. You can save and later reopen a project file and the movie will be in the same state of edit as it was when you saved it. A project is best described as a list of decisions that you've made about how to build your movie.

The project file holds all the information needed to create the finished movie. It includes links to the source files on the computer, where to start and stop each clip, and what effects, transitions, background music, and text to use.

> *Although it holds all the relevant information, a project does not contain copies of the source files, nor does it hold a copy of the finished movie.*

The ability to edit in such a way is termed **nondestructive editing**—the original video is not changed in any way. When you come to produce your final film, Movie Maker simply reads the list of instructions in your project file and **renders** a new video file by looking at (but not altering) all the other video clips it points to. Those clips are known as the **source files**.

Source files

The source files are multimedia files on your computer. They exist independently of Movie Maker and may be video files that you have captured from your camcorder or VCR, music files copied from your CDs, picture files from your digital still camera or scanner, and in fact almost any sound, video, or picture that you have on your computer.

It's good to check that your source files are on your hard drive(s) and in the folders you want them before you start work on a movie project. Move and rename any as needed before importing them into Movie Maker. If you move a file after it's been included in a project file, then Movie Maker won't be able to find it when it comes to render your film.

My Pictures   My Videos

My Music

> *If you have a choice, place multimedia source files on your fastest hard drive, preferably one that doesn't have your operating system on it. Movies place more demands on computers than other applications do, and this will help.*

Collections

Collections are **containers** for your clips; they are similar to folders and subfolders in Windows. Movie Maker uses the newer word "container."

The collections tree is in the **Collections pane** at the left. You can expand or contract any branch, just as you do folders or directories in Windows, by clicking the + or − icons.

Movie Maker starts with three collections that you cannot rename, move, or delete:

- ★ Video Effects
- ★ Video Transitions
- ★ Collections

Collections starts empty and waits for your collections to be added under it.

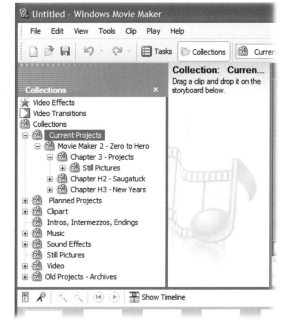

Creating new collections

Add collections one at a time by right-clicking an existing collection and choosing New Collection. Or use the menus and choose Tools > New Collection Folder.

You can then name it simply by typing in what you'd like to call it.

If later you would like to change the name of a collection, right-click it and choose Rename. You can then edit the name to suit. You can also rename by selecting a collection and pressing F2 or by using the menus, selecting the collection and going to Edit > Rename.

Copying collections

Within Movie Maker, you can copy a collection with all of its clips and paste it into another collection.

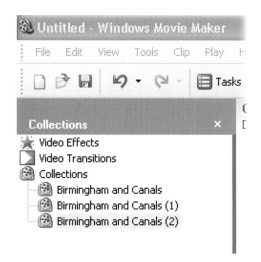

1. Simply right-click on a collection and select Copy (or select a collection and then Edit > Copy or select a collection and hit CTRL+C).

2. Then right-click on the collection container that you would like to copy the collection into and select Paste (or select a collection and then Edit > Paste or select a collection and hit CTRL+V).

If you paste a copy within the same container as the original, it'll give it the same name with a `(1)` behind it. A second paste will add a `(2)`, etc.

There is no way to drag and drop an entire folder of source files from another application, automatically adding a new collection complete with contents. You have to create a collection and import the files.

Organizing collections

Movie Maker sorts collection containers alphabetically, but you can still use your creativity to arrange your files. Here are some ideas about adding and arranging collections.

One approach is to sort them topically. For example, create a new collection named music, with collections under it for types of music, then artists, and under those a collection for each album with the files inside.

If the clips in the music collections are those you might use in movie projects, it helps to have them readily available to listen to. This helps you select some association between the music and a current or planned project.

Make a collection for special clips to use for beginnings, intermezzos (pieces used for intervals), and endings. A custom-made title from Photoshop would go into this collection, or a special video or image routinely used during closing credits.

Have three collections named Current Projects, Planned Projects, and Old Projects, with individual movie project collections inside them. You can easily grab a collection under Planned Projects and move to Current Projects when it's time to work on it, and then, when finished, move it to Completed Projects.

You can organize collections by moving them around in the collection tree. Drag and drop them to position them where you think best.

> *If you would like a collection container to appear further up the tree than it would by alphabetical order, you can add a space to the start of its name.*

It's best to copy clips from music or clipart collections and paste them into specific project collections. If you edit a clip so much that you need to start over, it'll be there in the topical collection to copy again. This is especially useful for large video files that you'll invest hours in dividing into clips. Clips in your collections take a very small amount of computer space because the source file is not copied.

Each time you start Movie Maker and go to the collection tree, you will see it fully expanded. A collapse all option would be nice but, as it is, a tree with few major branches can be collapsed with a few mouse clicks.

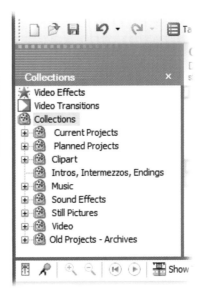

Add and organize collections to suit your personal needs and organization style. You might start with few collections and no need or desire to be organized. As your collections and their contents grow over time, you can reorganize them easily, without having to reimport source files.

Deleting collections

Deleting collections is easy: select one and press the DELETE key. It's almost too easy—Movie Maker doesn't ask do you really want to delete the whole collection?

> *Fortunately, you can use the* Edit > Undo *feature from the menu or press* CTRL+Z *to restore a deleted collection.*

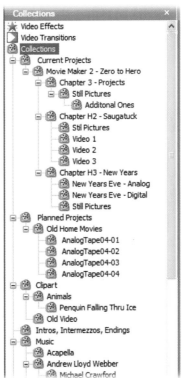

Do you share your computer?

Windows XP supports multiple users, each with their own desktop settings and preferences. Movie Maker stores a different collections file for each user, so if you would like someone to be able to view or edit your collections, they will have to use your desktop preferences.

Collections from Movie Maker 1

By default, the collections file from a previous release of Movie Maker is imported automatically the first time you start Movie Maker 2. To import another Windows Movie Maker 1 collections file (from another user):

1. Select File > Import into Collections.

2. In the Files of type: box, select Windows Movie Maker 1.x Collection Files.

3. Browse to the collection file you would like to use, select it, and then click Import.

The collections file is named `Windows Movie Maker.col` and is usually located in `C:\Documents and Settings\UserAccountName\Application Data\Microsoft\Movie Maker`. (UserAccount Name being the logon name of the user whose collections you want to import.)

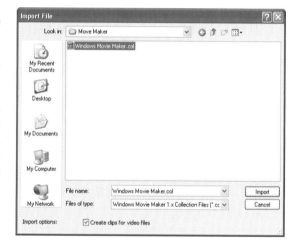

Clips within collections

Clips are the basic building blocks of movie projects. There are audio clips, video clips, still picture clips, and so on.

When you select a collection, the **thumbnails** or clip listing in the collection contents pane shows you the clips in that collection. Each thumbnail or item in the list is a clip.

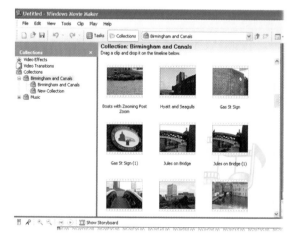

Clips are created by Movie Maker for imported files, video capture sessions, and narration recordings. Once created, there is a link between the source file on your computer and the clip's thumbnail. The linking information is maintained in the collections file.

> *Source files remain on your hard drive in their original locations; they do not get copied into Movie Maker, the collection database, or the working project.*

If you edit a source file in another program after it is already imported into your Movie Maker collection, the thumbnail will not change. Any changes *will* appear in previews and in any newly saved movie that uses the clip. Movies previously saved are not changed.

> *If you delete a thumbnail in Movie Maker, the source file remains unchanged and in its original location. It just isn't available to Movie Maker until you re-import it.*

Previewing clips

When you select a clip in the contents pane, it appears in the preview monitor. If it is a video or audio clip, double-clicking the thumbnail, or selecting the clip and pressing the space bar key, are easy ways to preview it.

You can't preview more than one clip at a time by selecting a group of them. The preview controls under the monitor appear unavailable if you select more than one thumbnail. These controls are covered in depth in **Chapter 5**.

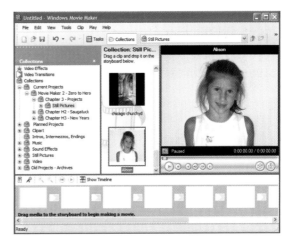

Clip duration

Each clip has a time dimension in addition to its other properties. When you preview a video clip, the numbers under the monitor at the right show the current position of the playhead within the clip and the total length of the clip. The time is in the format Hours:Minutes:Seconds:Hundredths of a Second (rather than the more usual H:M:S:Frames).

The zero position (00:00:00:00) is the start of the clip. When selecting a still picture to preview, the total length is indicated as zero.

Video source files have playing times (in length) before being imported or captured, although during editing, special effects can be applied to speed them up (to show a plant growing or a flower opening) or slow them down (to analyze a golf swing or watch a cheetah run).

Music selections are also time-based, even more so than video files. You usually play them in real time in your movies. You might clip them or fade them in and out, but you don't change the speed at which they play.

Still pictures don't have a time dimension as source files, nor when you import them into a collection. However, when you copy a clip to the storyboard/ timeline, it picks up a time dimension based on an option in Movie Maker.

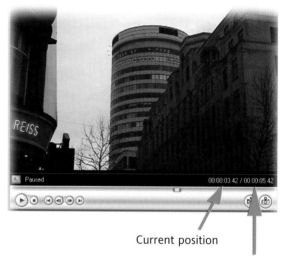

Current position

Total length

Viewing clip collections

Movie Maker provides two different views and six ways to sort clips in the collection contents pane. You can toggle between the **Thumbnails** and **Details** views by selecting one or the other from the drop-down menu.

The Details view most easily allows you to see a particular sort order. The six choices for sorting are Name, Duration, Start Time, End Time, Dimensions, and Date Taken.

Details view is particularly useful for music and audio files because the thumbnails are all the same, giving no additional information.

Thumbnail view is great for still clips because you see the picture on the thumbnail and the clips have no time dimension.

Toggling the view of video clips between Thumbnails and Details may be helpful in that you can see the first frame in the thumbnail view, to help you select appropriate clips, and see the length of each clip in the details view, which is helpful if you are looking for a 15-second video clip.

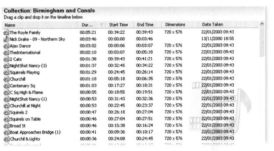

Changing the sort order

Once in the Details view, an easy way to change the sort order is to click on the sort option just above the list.

Select Duration at the top of the list to sort by duration, Name to sort by name, and so on.

Clicking the same sort option a second time will reverse the sequence of the listing, and the arrow will change from pointing up to down, or vice versa. Try it—it'll quickly become second nature.

Moving and copying clips

You can drag a clip from one collection and drop it onto another. Alternatively, you can use the standard Windows copy and paste keyboard shortcuts (CTRL+C to copy, CTRL+V to paste) to make as many copies as you want, either in one collection or different collections.

To select a number of clips in a collection and move or copy them at one time, you can select the first one and press the SHIFT key before selecting the last clip, thereby selecting all clips in between, too.

If the clips you want are not sequential, press the CTRL key as you select each of those you want. These are standard Windows shortcuts, so you may already be familiar with them.

Renaming or deleting clips

There are three ways to rename a clip:

★ Right-click on it and choose Rename from the menu. Then edit the name as necessary.

★ Select a clip and use the menu bar to choose Edit > Rename. Then change its name.

★ Select a clip and hit F2. This keyboard key is especially helpful and is standard across many Windows applications.

To delete a clip, select it and press the DELETE key.

As in most Windows applications, there are many ways to do the same thing. Some people prefer menu commands, others mouse commands, and others keyboard shortcuts. Use any of them or mix as you wish. Undo a deletion by using the Undo feature (undo also has the common CTRL+Z shortcut).

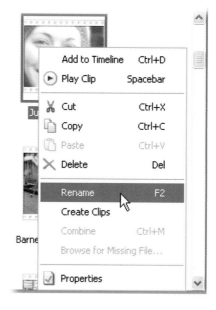

Relinking lost clips

If you rename or move source files on your hard drive(s), Movie Maker shows you a big red X as the thumbnail of any clip that refers to it.

You need to re-establish the link to the new file location:

1. Select the thumbnail in the collection contents pane.

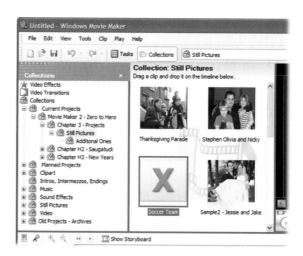

2. Select Browse for Missing File... either by right-clicking the thumbnail or from the Edit menu.

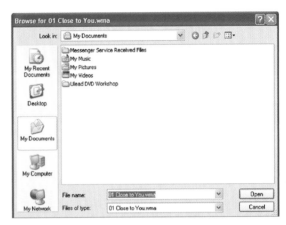

Movie Maker should now find and relink the clip for you automatically. If it can't, it will show you a file browser and allow you to search for the file yourself.

> It's a good idea to not move, rename, or delete the original source files until you're sure you've completed your work with them.

Creating Movie Maker 2 projects

In Movie Maker, a project begins when you create and save a new project file or add the first clip to the **storyboard** or **timeline**.

You may have been planning a movie project for a long time, taken video and still pictures, moved them into the computer as source files, created and arranged collections, selected appropriate background music, but this is the point when the actual *moviemaking* begins.

To start a new project:

1. Create a new project file by selecting File > New Project (or CTRL+N).

2. Select File > Save Project (or CTRL+S), which brings up a file dialog box.

3. Give your project file a name and save it in your preferred folder of project files. It is a good idea to use the default directory, which can help you remember where you've saved things.

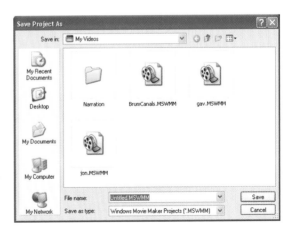

Movie Maker project files have a .MSWMM extension, and a new project file will always have that extension. As soon as you create a new file, the name of the new project shows up at the very top of the Movie Maker window.

Each time you save the project, any changes made to the storyboard/timeline are saved in the project file. Movie Maker will auto-save (creating a back-up copy) the project every 10 minutes but will not save changes you've made unless you save the project yourself. Use CTRL-S or click the disk icon on the toolbar to save. Save early and often.

The storyboard and the timeline

This is the core of Movie Maker, the place where you combine your creative ideas with the clips you select to turn them into reality. The area is displayed in either the more traditional storyboard view or the more digital-age timeline view. You can toggle back and forth between the two.

Moviemaking in Hollywood has a long tradition of using storyboards and timelines. In digital editing, the two are merging together. Some computer video software still uses separate windows for them, but Movie Maker nicely integrates the two.

Storyboard

Timeline

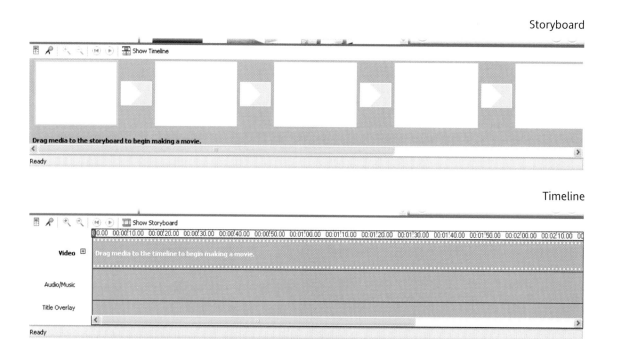

Most of the things you'll want to do can be achieved with either the storyboard or the timeline. Some things you can do in only one or the other. We'll look at those as we come to them.

During editing you will often toggle between the two views. Use the Show Storyboard/Show Timeline button (or CTRL+T) to change instantly and easily.

Storyboard view is great for when you focus on video clips and still pictures, selecting and sequencing them in the movie and applying transitions between them and video effects on them. Timeline view is best when you need to work with specific periods of time.

There are six icons above and to the left of the storyboard/timeline area. Place your mouse cursor over each and read the tool tip. The icons are the same in both storyboard and timeline views but appear unavailable when they're not applicable.

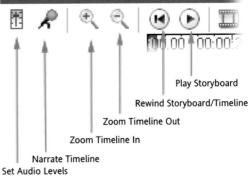

Play Storyboard
Rewind Storyboard/Timeline
Zoom Timeline Out
Zoom Timeline In
Narrate Timeline
Set Audio Levels

★ Play Storyboard/Timeline (CTRL+W)—previews the movie project starting where the playhead is located.

★ Rewind Storyboard/Timeline (CTRL+Q)—moves the playhead back to the start of the movie project.

★ Zoom Timeline Out/Zoom Timeline In (PAGE DOWN and PAGE UP keys as an alternate)—zooms in or out to focus on a specific part of the timeline, an overview of the entire project, or someplace in between. These are functional only in the timeline view.

★ Narrate Timeline—This opens a wizard, allowing you to record a commentary for your movie. This only works when in timeline view because audio tracks are not shown in storyboard view. If you click the button in the storyboard view, you'll be taken to timeline view. Narrating the timeline is fully covered in **Chapter 7**.

★ Set Audio Levels—Opens a window with the Audio Levels slider in it. This slider sets the relative balance between the audio on the video track and the audio/music track. When you narrate a movie or add backing music, you might want to raise the level of the commentary/music relative to the video sounds. This relative level setting applies to the entire project, not to particular clips. There are also clip-specific audio level settings to use. The overall audio level adjustment can be made at any time, even before any clips are added to the storyboard/timeline. Audio levels are fully covered in **Chapter 7**.

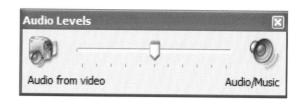

Using storyboard view

Storyboard view shows your project as a series of pictures, representing each clip—rather like a comic strip. Video clips are represented by a picture of their first frame, so this doesn't give a good impression of the length of each within your movie.

Adding clips to the storyboard

You drag in video and still picture clips directly from the Collection contents pane to the larger boxes on the storyboard. The storyboard fills in sequence from left to right. You can mix video clips and still pictures in any sequence.

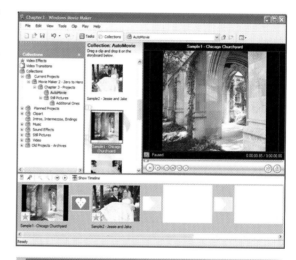

The name of the clip appears below it and the star box in the lower left corner of the clip represents any video effects that have been applied to the clip. The boxes between clip thumbnails represent transitions.

> *You can add effects on top of a clip only in the storyboard view and can add transitions only between pairs of clips.*

You can insert clips individually or select multiple clips in one collection and drag them as a group so that they will appear one after another.

You can add an entire collection by selecting one from the collection tree, in which case all the clips in its content pane will appear on the storyboard/timeline in a seemingly random sequence. In fact, the order is still pictures first, then video sequences in the order they were shot and captured—useful for viewing all your clips in sequence.

Reordering clips on the storyboard

You can change the order of clips by selecting one or more and dragging them to the new position on the storyboard. A blue line appears at the point that the clip(s) will be inserted. Clips after that in the storyboard (later in the movie) move to the right.

You can insert a clip at any point on the storyboard by dragging it from the collections pane. Drop another clip just in front of an existing one and it will inherit any transition, but not video effects, already there.

> *The clip that you place it on top of will move to the right—it will not be replaced or deleted.*

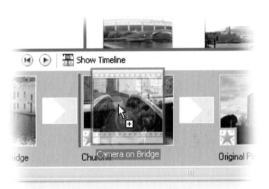

As usual, pressing the CTRL or SHIFT keys while selecting allows you to select multiple clips.

You can copy and paste clips in the storyboard in much the same way that you can in most computer applications: right-click them and use the context menu, select them and use the Edit menu, or use the keyboard shortcuts CTRL+C (to copy) and CTRL+V (to paste).

> *You can paste clips copied from the Collection contents pane into the storyboard, but you cannot paste clips from the storyboard into the Collection contents pane.*

Removing clips from the storyboard

Remove clips by selecting them and pressing the DELETE key—clips will move up the storyboard, filling in the gaps. The clips will not be deleted from the collection, just from that point in the movie project.

Alternate ways of removing clips are right-clicking on the selected clip(s) and selecting Delete from the context menu, or selecting the clips and choosing Edit > Delete.

If you right-click on a clip and select Cut (CTRL-X), it will be removed from the storyboard and placed into your clipboard.

To clear the storyboard completely and start over, select Edit > Clear Storyboard. Or right-click on the storyboard (not on a clip itself) and select Clear Storyboard. Or press CTRL+DELETE at any time.

Showing more or less of the storyboard

You can't select the size of the thumbnails on the storyboard directly, nor can you zoom in or out, but you can change them by dragging the horizontal divider bar between the storyboard and the upper panes of Movie Maker.

Grab it as you do when resizing a window and move it up or down for larger or smaller thumbnails. Larger ones may be appropriate when you're working on video effects or just want to see the thumbnails in more detail.

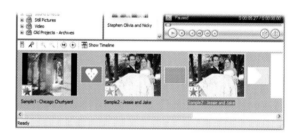

Smaller ones may be appropriate when you're moving clips from one position on the storyboard to another, or any other time you need to see more of the movie at once.

You can only size the clips up or down within limits, so you'll still need to scroll along to see all of a longer storyboard.

Previewing your movie with the storyboard

You should use the storyboard to look at the sequence of the clips and easily rearrange them and to select video effects and transitions. Most, but not all, of the information about the final movie is shown in the storyboard view.

Lingering over the star box will show you which effects are currently in place. The star turns blue. The transition thumbnail between two clips will show you the same thumbnail that you see in the transitions collection.

When you select a clip on the storyboard, the monitor reflects the entire storyboard and the selected clip in it.

Note in the picture to the right how the total time of the storyboard grows as clips are added. The time information in the preview monitor now shows the current position and total length of the movie project in the storyboard rather than the individual clip.

Although storyboard view doesn't have a time ruler like the timeline does, the tooltip when the mouse cursor is over a clip shows its time duration.

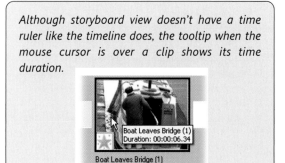

To watch a preview of the storyboard in the monitor, select any of the clips in the storyboard and press the space bar, or click the Play button under the monitor.

The preview will play from the starting point of the selected clip, not from the start of your movie project.

Although audio and narrative clips are not displayed in the storyboard, previewing plays the whole project, including video and audio.

Changing the default still picture duration

Still images have no time dimension associated with them as a clip in a collection. But they inherit the default time dimension as you drop them onto the storyboard/timeline.

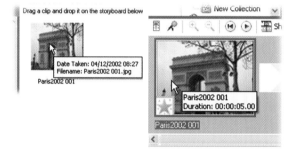

1. Select one of your still pictures and check the tool tip for the same clip in the collection contents pane and in the storyboard.

   The collection contents pane tool tip has no time dimension, whereas the same clip in the storyboard has a time duration—in this case, five seconds (00:00:05:00). You can edit their duration individually on the timeline as you can with any clip, which is explained later in this chapter.

2. Change the default duration by using the menu Tools > Options… and click on the Advanced tab.

3. The figure in the box after Picture duration: is the duration that still images are assigned when dragged on the storyboard/timeline. You can change it to anything in one-second increments from 1 to 30 seconds (use the up and down arrows next to the box).

4. Click OK. Test your new figure with a few images to ensure that you are comfortable with the setting before moving dozens or hundreds of them to the storyboard/timeline.

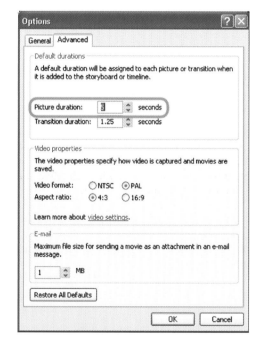

Using timeline view

When you toggle to the timeline view, you will see that the way the information about your movie project is displayed is different to storyboard view. This is because timeline view shows time information in much greater detail and also shows the details of the sound in your movie project.

The pane is split into tracks, showing the different components of the finished movie, video, audio/ music, and overlaid titles. The time ruler at the top shows which elements are positioned where. You can zoom in or out of the timeline by using the + and − magnifying glass icons. You can zoom between showing seven seconds to as much as three hours.

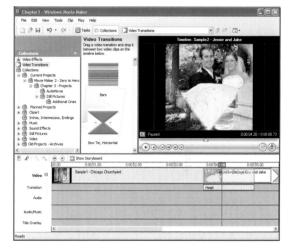

> *The* Video *track is composed of three separate elements, which you can expand or contract at will. You can click the + to the right of* Video *to expand or collapse the three video-related tracks.*

With the Video track expanded you can see five tracks in total:

★ Video—clips added to the project start at the left. You cannot have spaces between clips; if you delete one, the remaining will auto- matically move to fill the gap. Clips can overlap, however, if there is a transition added between them.

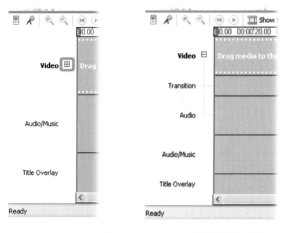

★ Transition—the timeline view of a transition, showing the name of the transition applied. The duration is determined by the amount of overlap between the two clips.

★ Audio—when a video clip includes audio, the audio part shows here. Right-clicking on the audio track provides options to Mute the audio, Fade in or out, or adjust the Volume of a clip.

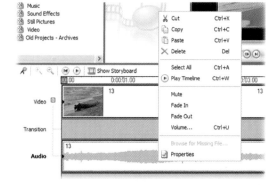

★ Audio/Music—this track is where a music selection or narration file is displayed. Within the clip display are both its name and a graphical representation of the sound. The graph shows volume levels within the audio clip. A portion of silence in the clip shows a single line. The louder the audio, the wider the graph.

★ Title Overlay—this track shows the position and duration of title overlays—the titles and credits you add to your movie. The titles do not appear in any collection once created; title information is embedded in the project file and not available as a source file for other projects.

You can adjust the various panes in Movie Maker to show more or less of a particular area. Moving the horizontal centerline of Movie Maker upward expands the height of the individual tracks, making it easier to see the audio graphs.

When working with audio and music tracks, it is helpful at times to see the variations in the sound as depicted in the graphical representation in the timeline. This helps when deciding where to clip it.

Adding video clips to the timeline

You add clips by dragging and dropping them from the Collection contents pane—into the appropriate track. The toggle button in Movie Maker makes it so easy to move between views that it's no longer a question of which view is best; it's more one of preference.

The name of the clip and the first frame are shown in a block in the Video track. The width of the block is determined by the duration of the clip—if you can't see the name or image, you have to zoom in on the timeline.

Any video effects added are represented by a blue star.

You can move them individually or select multiple clips in one collection and drag them as a group and they will appear one after another—just as in storyboard view.

Adding audio clips to the timeline

To add background music or any sound displayed as a clip in the Collection contents pane, simply drag and drop them in into the Audio/Music track.

Unlike with the Video track and video clips or images, it is possible to have a gap between clips (silence) in the Audio/Music track. This means you have more control over where you drag the clip to.

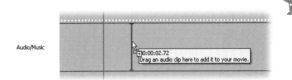

An audio clip dragged to an empty track will be positioned wherever it is when you release the left mouse button, leaving silence on either side.

> *You can drag video clips to the* Audio/Music *track instead of the* Video *track if you want— they will be treated as sound only and the images will not appear as part of your finished movie.*

The playhead will jump to the start of any added audio clip.

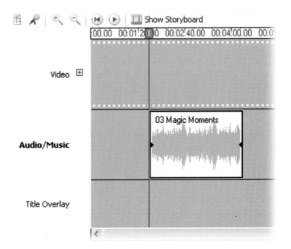

Reordering clips on the timeline

You have more control of the exact positioning clips in all the tracks on the timeline, as they can also be placed on tracks overlapping each other. This creates **transitions** between video clips and images and **fades** between sound clips. Fades and other types of transitions are explained in detail in **Chapter 4**.

You can pick them up (either from elsewhere on the timeline or from the Collection contents pane), and drop them in between other clips in a similar way to the storyboard. The blue I symbol appears at the point that the clip will be inserted and clips afterward move back in the timeline as they would in the storyboard.

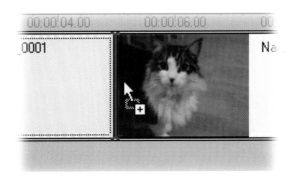

Overlapping clips on the timeline

If you drag a clip across another on the timeline, a dark blue wedge appears at the base of the clips. If you drop the clip at this point, the clips will overlap.

The clips are then displayed with the second faded above the first.

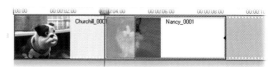

The fade will start to happen at the point that you position the second clip. If you overlap the clips more, the fade will take up a longer time in your movie.

The angle of the wedge indicates the speed of the fade, the rate at which the second clip will fade in over the top of the first.

Quick Fade

The duration of either clip is not altered, as two are playing at the same time the movie will be shorter, the longer the fade itself takes.

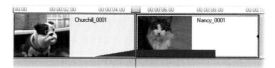

Slower Fade

The clip to the left (which will be played first) does not fade out as the second one starts. This is unimportant when dealing with video but matters more with sound clips.

Try it with two sound files and you will see that the sound graph of the clips stay as they were, rather than the sound levels of the second growing to full height over the duration of the fade.

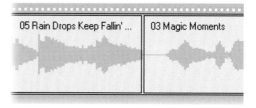

This means that for the duration of the overlap, both clips will play.

Transitions applied between video clips from the Video Transitions collection cause the same overlap, and are also shown by name in the Transition track. We'll show you how to add and manipulate these in **Chapter 4**.

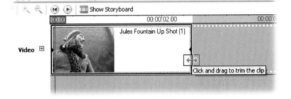

Trimming clips on the timeline

You can adjust the length of video and audio clips in the timeline view, trimming them to make them shorter. This is a good way of shortening your movie project without having to move or lose any clips.

Hovering your mouse pointer over the edges of a clip you've selected will change the pointer to double headed arrow. If you then click and drag the arrow, you can shorten the clip.

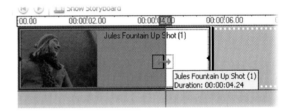

You can see how long the clip will be after you've trimmed it, as the area that will remain on the timeline is shaded blue as you drag. For the more mathematically minded, the duration in seconds is shown in the tooltip.

> *You can drag video or audio clips from either end, removing either the start or end of the clip. Still images only trim from their end in the timeline.*

When you release the mouse, the clip snaps to that length, and any video clips in the timeline afterward will move along with it. Again, audio clips won't move, leaving that portion of the track empty.

> *You can't trim the start of a clip that is the second in a transition; the red arrow doesn't appear.*

You can trim transitions themselves, if you have them applied and displayed in the expanded Transition track. The second clip moves back in the timeline.

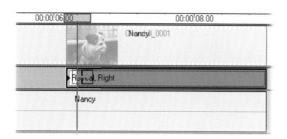

Previewing your movie with the timeline

You can watch a preview of your movie at any time. Simply press the space bar or click the Play button on the preview monitor and play will start from the position of the playhead.

Unlike in storyboard view, this could be at any point in the movie, not just in between individual clips. The preview monitor will show the same information—current time and total time of the movie project.

You can also watch your movie at almost any speed you like by dragging the playhead along the timeline. This is often called **scrubbing**. It's not an accurate way of judging the pace of your movie, but it's great for checking up on individual details. Zoom in and you can scrub slowly across a transition between two clips, watching how it looks frame by frame.

Just as on the storyboard, tooltips show you information, such as name and duration of clips, when you hover your pointer over them.

The AutoMovie wizard

Making an AutoMovie is the easiest way to create a new project. Select a collection or batch of selected clips and Movie Maker completely fills the storyboard/timeline for you. There are a number of styles that you can select, and the AutoMovie feature is a great way to create a movie project quickly that you can refine afterward.

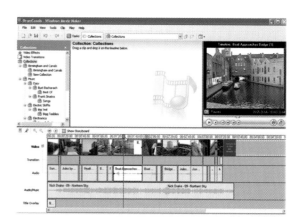

Making an AutoMovie

The AutoMovie wizard needs a collection that contains an audio clip more than 30 seconds long, or a number of video clips with audio that totals more than 30 seconds. If you try to run the wizard without enough clips selected you'll get an error message.

1. Place any clips you want in the movie into the collection and move any that you don't want out of it. A new current project collection specifically for the AutoMovie, with clips copied to it, may work best.

2. Instead of highlighting a collection, you could highlight selected clips within a collection and AutoMovie will use only those.

3. Once the collection or set of clips are selected, choose Tools > Auto Movie to begin.

4. Select one of the five styles:

★ Flip and Slide—flip, slide, reveal, and page curl video transitions are applied between clips. This works well for still image slideshows.

★ Highlights Movie—clean and simple editing with cuts, fades, a title, and credits. A quick way to create a basic movie project from a lot of clips.

★ Music Video—quick edits for fast beats and longer edits for slow beats. The clips are selected and edited in time to the music, perfect for when the music clip is the most important thing in your movie.

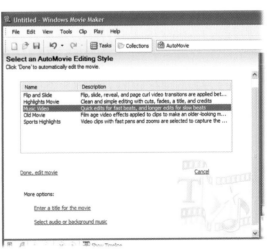

★ Old Movie—film age video effects applied to make an older-looking movie. Great for sentimental or comic effect.

★ Sports Highlights—video clips with fast pans and zooms are selected to capture the action, and an exploding title and credits are added at the beginning and end. Can quickly create a high-octane highlights movie, like you would see on a sports show.

There are two other options that you can use to select, edit, and re-edit as many times as you like.

5. The first, Enter a title for the movie, lets you add and edit a title for your movie. This overrides AutoMovie from using the name of the first clip as the title. Instead, it will appear as the title in the window title bar and in any titles Movie Maker adds to the project.

6. By choosing the second option, Select audio or background music, you can assign any of the audio files on your computer as background music. You can choose files from your default Movie Maker folder or Browse your computer for a music file that isn't in a collection.

> This is an exception to the rule that all source files for a project are first imported to a collection.

7. By moving the slider, you can adjust the audio levels in your movie. Where along the line you set this will depend on the type of movie you're creating: all the way to Audio/Music for a pop video and at various points toward Audio from video, depending on how much you want to hear the audio from your clips.

8. When finished with options, select Done, edit movie (or, if you've decided against an AutoMovie, click Cancel).

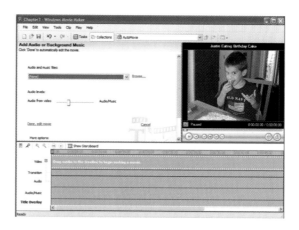

Once you've clicked on Done, AutoMovie will analyze the audio and the video clips, splitting the video by using scene changes within the clips. It will place multiple clips on the timeline from a single large video clip.

The sequence that clips appear on the timeline is determined by AutoMovie and will not align with any of the clip sorting choices in the Collection contents pane. It appears to put the video clips first, with still pictures following. It'll place the clips on the timeline complete with transitions, a title, and credits. If you didn't enter a custom title, it'll create one based on the name of the first clip on the timeline.

You can use the AutoMovie as your final project or as a starting point for editing. Save the AutoMovie project if you want, giving it a file name and location. Or clear the timeline and do it again with a different style. It's easy and fun.

Adding titles, transitions, and effects

Once you've assembled your clips in your movie project, either by hand or by using the AutoMovie, you will want to use the tools in Movie Maker to polish your movie. You can add titles and credits, transitions between clips, and video effects onto clips. Each is covered in its own chapter, but it's worth taking a brief look here as they're not separate things but parts of your movie project as a whole.

Titles and credits

Add text to your project by using Tools > Titles and Credits. Select the location of the text from the list of five options, fill in the desired text, choose an animation style, and click Done to add titles to the movie when finished.

Title animation choices are many, and third party tools will be providing additional ones.

Double-click an existing text item on the timeline and it'll reopen the Titles and Credits tool. You can easily edit the text or change the title animation style and font.

When a text clip is on the Video track, it has a plain background color. When it is used as a Title Overlay the background is transparent. Text clips are pretty versatile and can be edited on the timeline like any other.

Text in Movie Maker is fully covered in **Chapter 8**.

Video Effects

Movie Maker includes a number of video effects. The storyboard view is best for selecting and adding them, but you can use the timeline view if you prefer. Use the thumbnail view of its contents to see a brief view. Preview an effect by selecting a thumbnail and playing it in the preview monitor.

As you can see from the graphic, you can use your own image to preview the effect. Just replace the `sample1.jpg` file in the Movie Maker folder with one of your own.

Select any effect and drag it to the star box in the lower left corner of the video thumbnail on the storyboard.

Chapter 6 covers video effects fully and in detail.

Video Transitions

Unlike video effects that apply to just one clip, video transitions work with two adjacent clips. Video transitions are special effects used to move from one clip to the next. The storyboard is the easiest view to apply or change transitions, though using the timeline view is easier if you want to fine-tune the transitions.

Select the Video Transitions collection and use the thumbnail option to view the choices. Preview the transition by selecting a thumbnail and playing it.

Change a transition style by dragging a different one from the transition collection to the current transition. The new one will replace the previous, as there can't be more than one transition effect between two clips. They are not additive like video effects.

Video transitions are thoroughly covered in **Chapter 4**.

Saving and reviewing the project

You should have been saving your project over and over during editing sessions to make sure that it's worked, so it's time for one last review. Preview the entire movie and perhaps invite others to view it with you before saving the movie and burning a stack of CDs or DVDs.

Others will often catch things you've missed, like "My name in the credits is spelled wrong," for example. It's a great time to catch and fix things—this is where nonlinear editing really shines.
The options and process you go through to produce the final movie covered in **Chapter 9**.

Saving the movie project simply means that you are backing up the decisions you've made during editing in order to edit some more or produce the final move another time.

Project Properties

Before you save a movie project that you intend to generate and distribute, it's a good idea to review the project properties, which you can do by choosing File > Properties.

Entries in the Project Properties window are embedded in the movie you distribute and will be picked up when you search for projects by using Windows Explorer (or on the Internet, if the files are there). Windows Media Player will also display some of this information while playing your movies.

In the Project Properties window you can organize your projects according to title, author, and other fields. The fields in Project Properties follow:

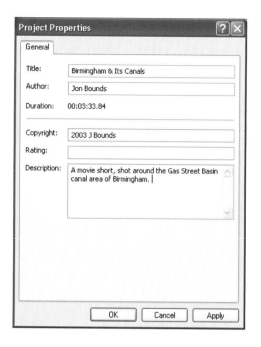

★ Title—By default, no title is entered. The title entered is the title for the final saved movie and is displayed by many media players when played. The maximum number of characters you can enter is 128.

★ Author—You can change the default author to another if you want. The name will be displayed by many media players when the movie is played. The maximum number of characters you can use for your author name is 128.

★ Duration—The length of the current Windows Movie Maker project is shown here. You cannot change this as it's calculated from the project itself by your computer.

★ Copyright—Copyright information is displayed by many media players when the movie is played. The maximum number of characters is 14, just enough for a year and a name.

★ Rating—The maximum number of characters is 20. You can include a cinema-style rating if you want.

★ Description—Any description may be entered for the current project and final saved movie. The maximum number of characters is 512.

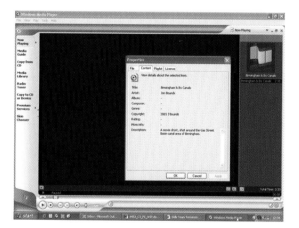

Click OK when you are happy with your entries in this window. They will be saved with the movie project and with the final movie when you decide it's finished. **Chapter 9** covers saving and distributing your finished movie.

The project properties can be seen by anyone who has the final movie because the project properties become the properties of the saved movie file. Don't enter personal information that you would regret sharing.

Transitions

In this chapter

A transition is a special video or audio effect that smoothes the sharp change between the last frame of one clip and the first frame of the next. In addition to simply smoothing what would otherwise be an awkward and abrupt change, a well-used transition can add meaning to a change of scene.

Movie Maker 2 includes a rich set of special video transitions and supports additional third party ones. They are simple to add, and you can control them to fit any style of movie you are making. In this chapter, we'll look at what types of transitions you can and would want to add to your own projects and how to apply them with finesse. This chapter covers the following topics:

★ The different types of video transitions
★ How transitions are used to further the story
★ The transitions available in Movie Maker
★ How to add transitions to your movie
★ Controlling the duration of transitions
★ Adding extra transitions

Types of transitions

Fades and wipes are the most commonly used video transitions, and you'll be familiar with them already, having seen them in film and on TV for years. These days, there are many variants on these themes, as computers have made them easy to develop.

Fades

A fade is a transition to or from a plain color or another scene, with one gradually turning into the next.

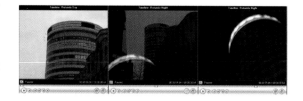

Fades often indicate a time change. A relatively short duration connotes a brief passage of time, while a longer one suggests a longer period. A fade may also indicate a change of location or subject matter. The duration of a fade should be consistent with the pace of the video.

Wipes

In a wipe, a new scene wipes away the previous one. Wipes were used a lot in silent films, but they lost much of their attraction as film audiences became more sophisticated. During the sound era they were mostly used in serials, low-budget thrillers, and promotion trailers. Since the 1970s, they have been used in comedies and tongue-in-cheek adventure films to create a period feeling or for comic effect.

Other types

Most other types are more noticeable to the viewer than either fades or wipes and are more specialized in their uses. Images wiping in intricate patterns or flipping and spinning round are rarely seen in movies these days, and are mostly only seen in pop videos or youth-orientated TV.

Examining how transitions are used

It's difficult to appreciate fully on the printed page just how different types of transitions have been used; we hope that the pictures and explanations here will suffice—along with your own experiences of film and TV.

If you'd like to watch the pieces we discuss here, they are available to view on the Internet.

The Internet Archive has hundreds of older movies that are beyond their copyright time and are free to download and use. They include more than 1,200 advertising, educational, industrial, and amateur films made from 1927 through to the present day. The web site is
http://webdev.archive.org/ movies/.

Let's look at one piece to see how transitions were used.

A 1958 documentary about the first trans-Atlantic jet flight, from New York to London (*6-1/2 Magic Hours*), runs 12-1/2 minutes.

It opens with a fade from black and follows with a half-dozen fades, using various clips of white fluffy clouds. It then fades to black over the titles to transition to another location—scenes of people in New York.

After that, it fades to a clip of the airport runway, fades to clouds again, and uses a number of fades when changing points of view as the subject of weather reporting is covered. There is then a transition from black that uses the shape to zoom in to a weather map.

In flight, it fades from the plane's exterior to inside. The movie's body during the flight uses mainly straight cuts.

Toward the end, it fades to an exterior scene of the landing in London, then fades to scenic clips of London, which fade back to the airplane exterior in flight. The movie then fades to Paris and the Eiffel Tower, then back to the airplane, then to the sky with ending text credits, and finally fades to black at the end.

When to use transitions

Use transitions with restraint. You want your viewers to enjoy your video and still pictures. They know that computers can make really neat effects and will quickly tire of watching the same ones over and over. The primary purpose of a movie is not to demonstrate your computer's capabilities or your use of it, but to communicate and share your special and personal video and pictures.

Experienced storytellers don't often use transitions; they prefer to keep the story moving with straight cuts. Some editors use fades to mask poor footage, insufficient material, directional changes, missing scenes, and other shortcomings.

Use transitions to blend title and credit text, suggest feelings of space or time, or denote a flashback. Use them also in short montage-type videos, such as television commercials, to blend together a number of short scenes of varied subject matter into a smoother visual production.

It is common and appropriate to use many neat transitions between pictures in a slide show. They lack the visual and audio richness of a movie. If you are moving from slide shows to video editing, be careful not to carry forward your frequent use of distracting transitions.

Transitions in Movie Maker 2

Movie Maker provides 60 video transitions. Select the Video Transitions collection, and the thumbnails (or the listing, depending on which view you have selected) of the transitions will appear in the Collections content pane.

The Microsoft Plus! Digital Media Edition, which you can purchase from Microsoft, offers an additional 25 transitions, and third-party packs are available as well.

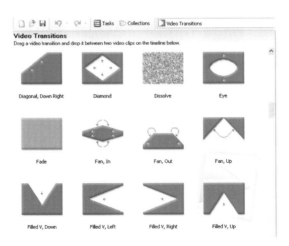

Previewing transitions

You can get a good idea of what each transition will look like from its icon. The blue portion is the first image and the white is the second, and the arrows represent the movement. But of course you can't really see without movement. Preview a video transition by selecting it in the Collection contents pane and pressing the space bar or clicking on the Play button in the preview monitor.

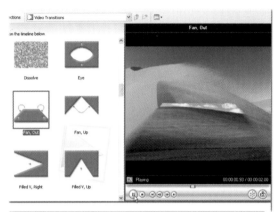

The preview uses two sample still images that come with Movie Maker. Without a powerful computer, you cannot always use Movie Maker to preview transitions between moving images in real time, so it uses still images so you can view them as easily as possible.

You can use your own images instead. To look best, they should be 320x240 JPG files with 16 million colors or landscape mode images with a 4:3 dimension ratio.

If you would like to, open the `c:\Program Files\ Movie Maker\Shared` folder. The images that Movie Maker uses are: `sample1.jpg` and `sample2.jpg`.

Rename the originals to something like `sample1original.jpg` and `sample2original.jpg`, and substitute your pictures, saving these as `sample1.jpg` and `sample2.jpg`.

If you want to change back, rename the originals to `sample1.jpg` and `sample2.jpg` again.

A good way to see quickly different transitions in action is to use the down-arrow key to move from one transition to the next in the collection, pressing the space bar on each. The preview monitor will show each transition as you go.

Movie Maker 2's standard transitions

It's not always possible to see the complete list of transitions at one time in Movie Maker, no matter how you resize the windows—so they are all overleaf, for reference.

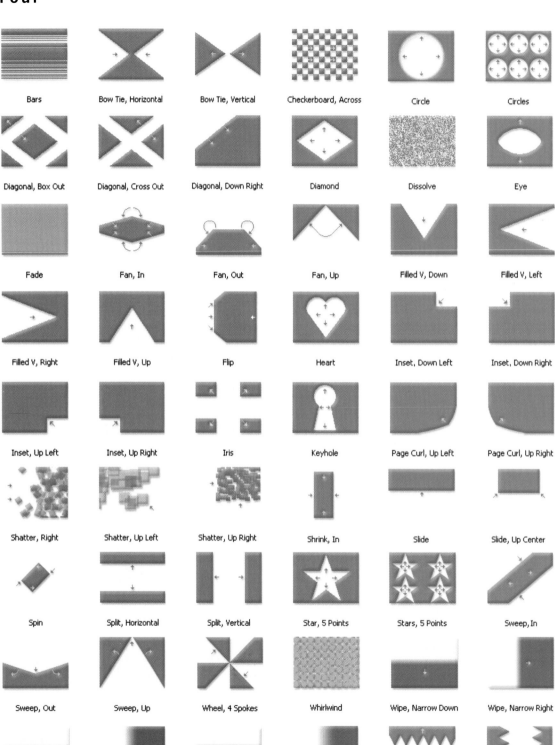

★ **Four**

Bars	Bow Tie, Horizontal	Bow Tie, Vertical	Checkerboard, Across	Circle	Circles
Diagonal, Box Out	Diagonal, Cross Out	Diagonal, Down Right	Diamond	Dissolve	Eye
Fade	Fan, In	Fan, Out	Fan, Up	Filled V, Down	Filled V, Left
Filled V, Right	Filled V, Up	Flip	Heart	Inset, Down Left	Inset, Down Right
Inset, Up Left	Inset, Up Right	Iris	Keyhole	Page Curl, Up Left	Page Curl, Up Right
Shatter, Right	Shatter, Up Left	Shatter, Up Right	Shrink, In	Slide	Slide, Up Center
Spin	Split, Horizontal	Split, Vertical	Star, 5 Points	Stars, 5 Points	Sweep, In
Sweep, Out	Sweep, Up	Wheel, 4 Spokes	Whirlwind	Wipe, Narrow Down	Wipe, Narrow Right
Wipe, Normal Down	Wipe, Normal Right	Wipe, Wide Down	Wipe, Wide Right	Zig Zag, Horizontal	Zig Zag, Vertical

Manipulating transitions

Movie Maker's transition effects are of high quality; you should have no difficulties selecting appropriate transitions for your movies. You can apply them in either storyboard or timeline views.

Transitions in storyboard view

To use a transition in a project, it's easiest to start in the storyboard view with the Video Transitions collection showing and your project open.

1. Preview available transitions, and select the one that will work best between your two clips.

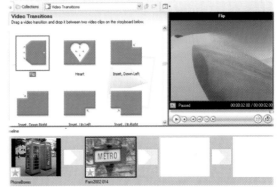

2. Drag and drop the transition icon from the collection contents pane to the small transition box between two clips.

The transition box will alter to display the icon of the applied transition. You can then preview the storyboard and see the transition in action.

Paris2002 014

> *To remove a transition in storyboard view, simply select it in its box between clips and press* DELETE *(or right-click the transition and choose* Delete*).*

If you drag and drop a transition between clips that already have one applied, the previous style will be completely replaced. There can only be one transition style between two clips.

> *You cannot alter the duration of a transition in storyboard view.*

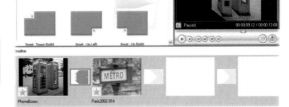

Transitions in timeline view

You can add a transition between clips just as easily as in the storyboard view, but depending on your zoom settings and the length of your clips, it can be difficult to see exactly the effect your transitions will have.

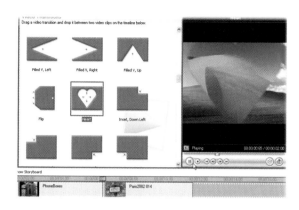

1. In the timeline view, select your transition and drag it from the collection contents pane to the point at which your two clips join.

Transitions are displayed and manipulated in their own track in timeline view; it is linked to the Video track. The three linked video tracks can be expanded or contracted. When contracted, you see only the Video track; when expanded, you additionally see the associated Transition and Audio tracks. If you drag a transition effect into the timeline when the tracks are contracted, it'll automatically expand the view.

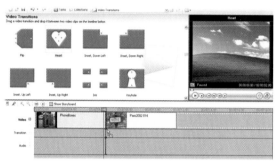

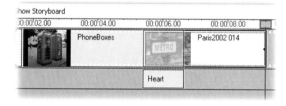

2. The transition will appear as a block between the two clips, in the Transition track underneath. The duration of the transition is shown by both the length of this block and by the amount that the clips in the Video track overlap. The type of transition applied is indicated by its name.

To see this in detail, it may be necessary to zoom in on the timeline.

3. You can preview the transition either by playing the movie in the preview monitor or by dragging the playhead along the timeline where the two clips overlap.

To remove a transition in timeline view, simply select it on the Transition *track and press* DELETE *(or right-click the transition and choose* Delete*).*

As in storyboard view, there can only be one transition style between two clips. A second added will replace any previously applied.

Changing the duration of transitions

Along with the style of transition you choose, the other main area of control is altering the amount of time that it takes for one clip fully to become another. This can radically alter the pace and feeling of your movie.

Setting the default transition duration

Transitions applied in either view will take on the default length that Movie Maker currently has set. You can alter individual transitions in timeline view, but it can be useful to set a default duration for an individual project, particularly if you are going to be using a lot of transitions.

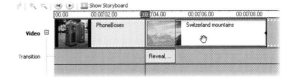

1. To change the default transition duration, select Tools > Options and click on the Advanced tab.

2. To alter Movie Maker's default transition length, use the up and down arrow buttons to the right of Transition duration:, you cannot type a value directly into the box.

Movie Maker will allow you to select default transition lengths between 0.25 seconds and 5 seconds, in 0.25 second intervals.

Altering a transition from the Video track

You can alter the amount of time a transition takes to complete, either lengthening or shortening it by manipulating clips in the Video track on the timeline.

To do so, simply pick up the second clip of a transitioned pair by clicking and dragging it. You can drag the clip left or right, increasing or decreasing the amount of time the transition will take.

The blue wedge shows the amount of each clip that will be visible over the time for the transition.

You can extend the transition for the entire duration of the second clip, giving the most gentle transition possible.

> *If you continue to drag the second clip so its end would be before the end of the first clip, the transition is removed from the timeline.*

You can shorten the transition all the way down to one frame (which is 12 hundredths of a second long in Movie Maker).

> *If you drag the start of the second clip right past the end of the first, the transition is removed.*

As discussed in **Chapter 3**, if you drag one clip over another in the video track, it will create a fade between the two. This will appear in the Transition track, just as if you'd added a Fade from the Video Transitions collection.

Altering transitions in the Transitions track

You can also manipulate the transitions themselves in their track on the timeline. You can only shorten them here, however; you cannot increase them in duration.

Click and drag the clip handle on the left-hand side of the transition clip to the right. A tooltip gives you the new duration of the transition.

> *The second clip in the transition (and any subsequent clips in the timeline) are pushed back—they do not have their length altered in any way.*

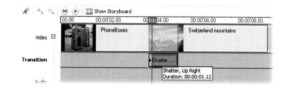

Fades to or from plain color

Video transitions have to be applied between two clips. To fade in or out to black or white on just one clip, Movie Maker includes video effects, but the effects occur in less than a second and can't be controlled.

For a longer fade or one that holds on the color before or after the clip, you have to use a little ingenuity.

1. First, you have to make your own plain black or white (or whatever color you want) image. You can use any image editing program you want. Microsoft Paint, included with Windows, is suitable and can be found at Start > All Programs > Accessories > Paint.

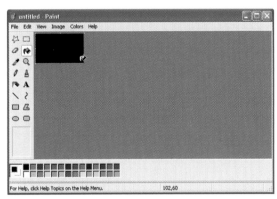

2. Create a new image and fill it with your chosen color, then save it somewhere you can easily find it on your hard drive.

It's not important what file name you give the image or what type of file you save it as, as long as Movie Maker can import it (commonly supported formats include JPEG, GIF, PNG, and Paint's default format, BMP).

3. Close your paint application and get back into Movie Maker. Import your plain image (File > Import into Collections...) and place it into an appropriate collection folder.

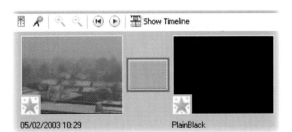

4. Drag your plain image into the timeline/storyboard before or after the clip you want to fade.

5. Apply a fade transition between your clip and the plain image. You can do this by dragging one from the Video Transitions collection or simply by dragging the appropriate clip across on the timeline.

6. Now, adjust the duration of the fade until you're happy with the effect.

A fade in from black is a normal and good way to start a video. It can help with sound also, if you want to start the audio before the video begins. Once you've created the plain images, you can use them in any project you like.

Using transitions creatively

If you focus on the transitions and demonstrating your computer's capabilities, you may not notice that, beyond a certain point, additional transitions detract from the basic message of the movie. Overusing transitions is a sure way to kill the feelings of professionalism that the viewers have gotten from your well-edited video. Here are a couple of uses to get you started on the right track.

Fade from black with audio

You can use a traditional fade in from black at the beginning of a video simply to get things started smoothly. Starting the sound slightly before the picture appears gives a nice lead-in.

1. Add a plain black image to the storyboard/timeline followed by an introductory clip.

2. Create a smooth fade between the two by dragging the clip over the plain image.

3. Drag your background music into the Audio track, positioning it at the beginning of the black image to begin to set the mood with the audio a couple moments before the first image is seen.

Fun transitions between similar images

You can use some of the more spectacular transitions for fun.

A friend Leo wanted to give his mother something special for Mother's Day and chose to give her a picture of himself as "Mona Leo". Putting the original Mona Lisa on the timeline, followed by Mona Leo, seemed to warrant a transition. The classic fade and other softer ones worked but lacked a sufficient "fun factor."

One of the shatter transitions (Shatter, In) was selected to make a more dramatic statement. A subtle transition might leave the viewer not noticing the change.

A good place to practice using transitions is on introductory and closing clips. The mixture can be as artistic or offbeat as you want, and here it need not distract from the main body of the video.

Audio transitions

Overlapping video clips for a fade will also overlap and fade the audio tracks connected to them. You can also overlap clips in the Audio/Music track the same way you overlap video clips, grabbing the right one and dragging it over the one to its left.

Audio, when started earlier than the video of a clip, can raise the viewer's expectation of an upcoming scene. When audio is carried a bit into a following scene, it can reinforce and carry the message of the first clip, binding the two clips together in the viewer's mind. Such audio transitions can be very effective in achieving a finely polished result.

Chapter 7 covers the use and editing of audio in Movie Maker in great detail. When you assess a project to determine when to add a video transition, think about adding audio transitions also. Sound and video should not always be edited in a parallel manner.

Getting more transitions

If the 60 video transitions that come with Movie Maker are simply not enough, or you need a specific transition that is not available, then there are additional transitions available. Some you will have to buy, but Microsoft, or some other philanthropists, may produce extra transitions that are free to download.

Go to Help > Windows Movie Maker on the Web to open your browser and go to Microsoft's web site for Movie Maker information. The site links to both Microsoft's effect and transition packs and third-party software.

Pixelan (see www.pixelan.com), one third-party developer, has so far released three transition packages for Movie Maker. They are available in fully functional, free demo versions (though admittedly the demo version embeds a big X along with each included transition until you pay up).

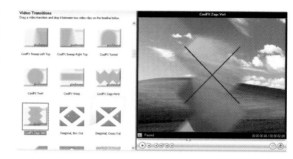

After installing and restarting Movie Maker, the third-party transitions will show up in the Video Transitions collection alongside those that came with Movie Maker and will work in exactly the same way.

Movie Maker needs additional computer memory when extra transitions are added. The extra memory used when all three Pixelan transition packages are installed, for example, is about 8MB. If you have lots of RAM, this is a modest amount. If you are trying to minimize memory demands, you can move the packages out of the Movie Maker Shared subdirectory after installing and reviewing them, and then copy them back for sessions that use them.

Editing clips

In this chapter

Clips are the basic building blocks of movie projects: they are imported into a collection and moved into the storyboard/timeline to form the basis of your movie. As well as the control you have over them as part of a project, which is covered in **Chapter 3**, you can also split, combine, and otherwise manipulate clips themselves.

In this chapter, we'll go deeper into using clips. We'll explore why, when, and how to manipulate clips further in a collection or on the timeline of a project. Not only that, we'll trim and nudge clips on a timeline to further your understanding of how to fine-tune your movie projects. This chapter will cover the following topics:

★ The differences between clips in collections and in movie projects
★ Splitting clips, combining them, and taking still images
★ Trimming clips on the timeline and using the preview monitor
★ Nudging clips on the timeline and fine-tuning transitions
★ Copying and pasting clips both in one project and between different movie projects

Understanding clips

When you select a collection, the thumbnails or listing in the collection contents pane shows the clips in it. There is a link between the source files on your computer and the clips in your collections. This information is stored in the Movie Maker collections file, a personal database for each computer user.

When you select a clip in a collection, it previews in the monitor. You can see a still picture, watch a video clip, listen to music, or hear a narrative. Double-click a thumbnail (or select a clip and press the space bar) to preview it.

Because project files are independent from the collections, you can view collections as stepping stones to getting clips into projects. Once they make it to the storyboards/timelines, the clips in the collections are technically no longer needed. Save them in the collections only if you want to use them further in current or future projects.

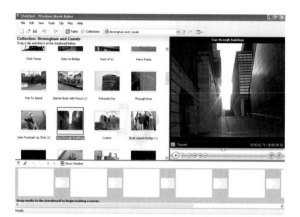

Clips in collections and in a project

Let's go through a hands-on exercise to help solidify your current understanding of clips in collections versus clips on the storyboard/timeline and to learn more about how to handle them in the two different places. Sometimes starting Movie Maker and experiencing it is easier than learning about it by reading. In the case of editing clips, a hands-on tutorial approach might be best.

First we'll study a clip for a bit, and then we'll split it in a number of different ways.

1. Start by making a new test collection with a single video clip in it. We've used a WMV source file that had several different scenes and was more than two minutes long.

2. Then start a new project (no need to save it) and drag the clip onto the timeline.

3. Select the clip in the collection. Note that the name of the clip shows above the monitor and the monitor's seek bar is all the way to the left at the zero position.

> *The seek bar always starts at or returns to the clip's zero position when a clip in a collection is first selected.*

4. Select the same clip in the timeline. Note that the name of the clip above the monitor is now preceded by the word Timeline, and the seek bar is at the same location as the timeline playhead.

> *Move the seek bar or playhead and see that the other moves also. They are linked to each other in terms of position within the clip.*

5. Leave the seek bar and playback indicator at about the midpoint of the clip's duration.

6. Now toggle to the storyboard view. Note that the position of the seek bar and playback indicator stays at the location it was when you left the timeline view.

> *The storyboard and timeline views are alternate views of the same information about the clips in the project—which is not the same as clips in a collection.*

7. Toggle back and forth between the storyboard and timeline views a couple times and see that the position remains the same in each view.

8. Select the clip in the collection again. Note that the position of the playback indicator on the timeline doesn't change, but the position of the seek bar goes to the zero point again.

The monitor is now previewing the clip selected in the collection. It is no longer previewing the clip on the timeline. Although they start off as identical clips from the same source file, you can start to see that they're now independent.

9. With the test clip in the collection selected, move the seek bar to about the 1/4 point and split the clip by clicking the Split Clip button under the monitor.

You now have two clips in the collection but still one clip in the timeline. The first part of the clip retains the clip's name and the other part is assigned the same name but followed by (1). In the collection details view, you see that the durations of the two clips correspond to their split durations.

The clip on the timeline hasn't changed by splitting the clip in the collection. It has the same name as the first of the two clips in the collection.

10. Select the clip on the timeline and move the seek bar or playhead to about the 3/4 point of the clip's duration. Split it like you did the clip in the collection, by using the same Split Clip button.

You now have two clips on the timeline, each with the same name. Note that the clip name above the monitor does not show a (1) suffix on the second clip in the timeline to distinguish it from the first. All splitting on the timeline results in different but identically named clips.

A clip in the timeline, although it came from a clip in a collection, is no longer related to it. You are free to edit (or delete!) each completely separately.

Why split clips in collections?

You may want the clips in the collection to be around for a while, to use later in the same project or different ones. There are a number of reasons to do this. You can always import the source file again to get another copy of the clip but, if you have manually split and renamed clips in a collection, you might not want to repeat the process for another use of a clip.

Try to rename a clip on the timeline. You can't. You have to live with whatever name was on the clip when it initially moved from the collection to the timeline. This is a good reason to think about the clip's name while it is in the collection. During project editing sessions, it's nice to have meaningful names to work with.

If your current project is somewhat experimental and you clear the timeline to get a fresh start on the movie, you might want the clips handy to add back into the timeline.

The decision about when to delete the clips in a collection, and the collections themselves, is yours to make. Keep them at least until you have saved your final movie.

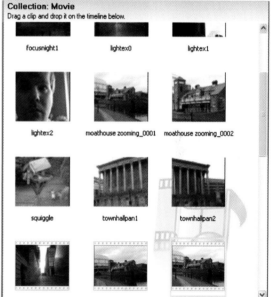

Splitting and combining clips

Most of the ways that you can edit clips can be performed in either the collection or the timeline. As a general rule of thumb, if you're editing the clips before you know exactly how you'll use them in the movie, then altering clips in the collections contents pane is the place to be. If you just want to fine-tune your movie, then you should use the clips already in the timeline.

> *Clips can be dragged and dropped from a collection to a timeline. Try dragging and dropping the clip from the timeline back to the collection. It can't go that way. It's a one-way street.*

Automatic clip creation

If you have chosen not to allow Movie Maker to create clips when you've captured or imported your video, you can always run the clip creation function on clips in your collections.

Right-click on a clip and choose Create Clips from the menu.

The automatic clip creation function of Movie Maker will go into effect, detecting changes of scene in order to split the clip. The created clips will appear in the collection contents pane.

> *This automatic clip creation process is not available for a clip on the timeline. In a project, you can split a clip manually but not automatically.*

Movie Maker always uses the same criteria for automatically creating clips, which means that if you import or capture the same video at different times and then create clips, you will always end up with identical clips in the collection. This also means that attempting to create clips from an automatically created clip will not produce further subdivision of clips.

Splitting clips manually

You can split clips either on the timeline or in a collection, but remember that changes made to one will not affect the other. To **split** a clip:

1. First, select the clip you'd like to divide, in either the Collections contents pane or in the storyboard/timeline. It will appear in the preview monitor.

2. Use the seek bar or the Play/Pause button to find the place in the clip at which you'd like to make the split. You can adjust the position with frame accuracy by using the Previous and Next Frame buttons.

3. When you're happy with the exact position to split, click on the Split Clip button, and Movie Maker will divide your clip into two.

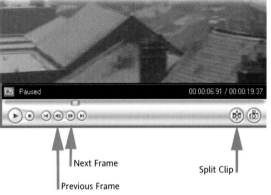

Paused   00:00:06.91 / 00:00:19.37

Next Frame

Previous Frame

Split Clip

A clip split in the collections contents pane will become two clips. The first half will have the same name as the original clip, and the clip starting from the split point will have the same name—but with (1) appended to it.

Any changes made to a clip in the collection will not affect copies of that clip already in the storyboard/timeline.

Split a clip on the timeline and you will have two clips with the same name, one sitting after another in the timeline.

In fact, splitting a clip in the timeline will make absolutely no difference to your movie, unless you then make a change to one of the clips. You can move, copy, or delete either of the clips—as is fully explained in **Chapter 3**.

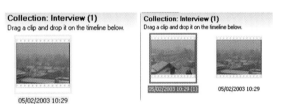

Collection: Interview (1)
Drag a clip and drop it on the timeline below.

05/02/2003 10:29

Collection: Interview (1)
Drag a clip and drop it on the timeline below.

05/02/2003 10:29 (1)   05/02/2003 10:29

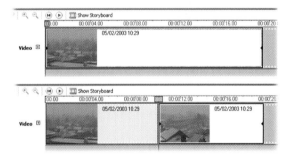

Combining clips

Of course, you can use the Undo feature of Movie Maker to reverse a split that occurred recently. You can also combine two or more clips that were originally split in either the collection or the timeline.

> *To combine clips, they must have been previously split and you must combine them again at the same points. You cannot combine two unrelated clips or two ends of a clip after you have discarded the middle section.*

Select the clips you want to combine. Once selected, use Clip > Combine (or Ctrl+M).

You can right-click on selected groups of clips in the collection contents pane and choose Combine, but you cannot do this in the timeline/storyboard.

Taking a still image from a clip

You can use Movie Maker to take a still picture from any video clip. This can be useful to create special transitions or freeze-frame the action—or simply to edit or print out your favorite snapshot of the action in an image editing program.

1. Simply preview the clip, either from the storyboard/timeline or its collection, and use the playback controls to pause the clip on the frame that you'd like to use as a still picture.

2. Click on the Take Picture button at the bottom right of the preview monitor.

A file browser window will open, prompting you to save the image. You can only choose to save the picture as a JPEG image. It will be saved at the same size as the video clip and with maximum JPEG quality.

3. Choose a location and a file name for your work and click Save.

Movie Maker will save the picture onto your hard drive (or anywhere else you select) and also automatically import it as a still picture with that name to whatever collection you have selected.

You can now use that picture as any other in your movie projects.

Because Movie Maker has also saved the picture onto your computer, you can open and use this in any program that supports JPEG images—but remember that altering the image file itself, moving it or deleting it, will change how Movie Maker can use it.

Collection: Movie

Drag a clip and drop it on the storyboard below.

Julia   Movie _1__0001

Trimming clips

Trimming clips is an important step toward making a movie flow smoothly. Trimming can only be done in the timeline view of a project.

When you split a clip, the parts of the clip that are separated by the split are no longer available to you when fine-tuning the clip later. When you trim a clip, all frames stay available to the clip, but some appear and others are hidden. You set the dividing points by selecting the clip's **Start** and **End Trim Points**— changing the location of the dividing lines between the hidden and appearing frames.

Fine-tuning the location of the trim points is done in timeline view and can be controlled right down to the divisions between individual frames. You can trim a clip from either the left or right ends, or both.

Trimming clips in the timeline

When you select a clip in the timeline, note the little black pointers on the left and right edges. These are called **trim handles**. You can grab either handle and pull it to trim the clip.

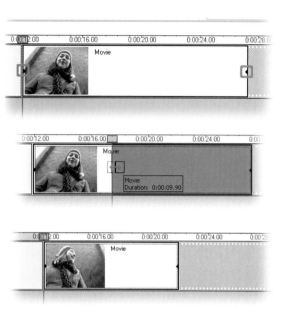

Hover over a trim handle with your mouse and the tooltip says "Click and drag to trim the clip." That's exactly what you do. The blue portion indicates what will be the viewable frames when you let go of the mouse button. The tooltip tells you the duration of the clip between its trim points.

In the Video track, clips will close in on the timeline. For more information about the behavior of clips on the Video and other tracks, see **Chapter 3**.

Trimming by using the preview monitor

A better way to trim a clip than grabbing and pulling the trim handles is to use the playback controls of the monitor to go to the exact point where you want to trim the clip, moving one frame at a time if needed. This allows you more exact control over the start and end trim points.

When the seek bar is where you want the trim point to be, choose Clip > Set Start Trim Point (or press CTRL+SHIFT+I). When the playback indicator is at the point where you want the selected video or audio clip to stop playing back, choose Clip > Set End Trim Point (CTRL+SHIFT+O).

Altering trim points

To clear the trim points on a clip and start over, select the clip in the timeline and choose Clip > Clear Trim Points (CTRL+SHIFT+DEL). You can also clear the trim points by dragging both trim handles back again to the ends of the clip.

When you select a clip on the timeline that has been trimmed, the time scale above it is gray to the left and right of the clip, giving you visual clues about how much of the clip is currently hidden by the trimming. In the gray areas are frames that can be revealed again by dragging the trim handles.

Moving clips on the timeline

As learned in **Chapter 3**, you can move clips around the timeline and storyboard much as you can move text around in a word processor by clicking and dragging or copying and pasting.

If you move or copy clips on the timeline, you move or copy all Movie Maker's information about how they are being used—including trim points and any effects applied to them.

Nudging clips

You can nudge a clip or a group of clips to the left or right on the timeline, one frame at a time. This is useful to control just how much of a clip is overlaid on an adjacent one and is used in a transition.

Select the clip(s) to nudge and from the Clip menu, choose Nudge Left (CTRL+SHIFT+B) or Nudge Right (CTRL+SHIFT+N). If either option appears unavailable, then the clip is at the end of where it can be nudged.

Clips that are not overlaid as part of a transition can only be nudged left (creating a Fade transition, much as dragging it left would). Nudging left extends the duration of a transition; nudging right shortens a transition.

Copying clips within a project

You can copy a clip or multiple clips on the timeline. The clips can be adjacent or separated by other clips.

For a group of adjacent clips, press the SHIFT key to anchor the first selected clip as you then select the last clip with the mouse. Once selected, use CTRL+C to copy them to the computer's clipboard. You can also click and drag a dotted rectangle around groups of clips to select them—as you can with folders and icons in Windows.

For nonadjacent clips, select the first clip and press the CTRL key as you select additional clips. Again, use CTRL+C to copy them to the clipboard.

Clips that are selected in the storyboard view, including transitions, are outlined by a blue rectangle.

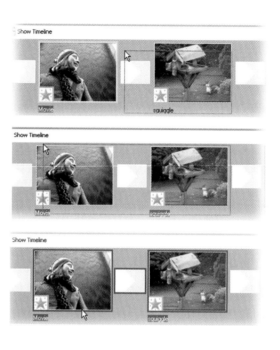

Video effects applied to the clips will be copied with them. If you copy multiple adjacent clips, the transitions between them will also be copied. If you select nonadjacent clips, transitions are not copied.

Move to the point in the storyboard/timeline where you want to place the new copies, and paste them with CTRL+V.

It's a bit easier to copy and paste clips in the storyboard view. When it is time to paste, select any clip on the storyboard and the pasted ones will go in front of the selected clip. You can select the first unused clip space to paste them at the end of the existing clips.

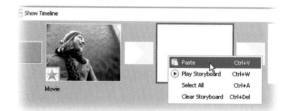

You can't copy clips and title overlays at the same time, but you can copy a set of video clips and then go back and copy a set of title overlays.

All copies of clips have the same names as the originals, durations, effects, and trim points. But they are independent of each other and can be further edited and used in the project. You can do a lot with them, but you can't rename them.

Copying clips between projects

You can even copy a clip or multiple clips, complete with effects and transitions, across projects.

1. Open one project, select the clips from the storyboard/timeline, and copy them (CTRL+C) to the computer's clipboard.

2. Open another project and paste them (CTRL+V) into the storyboard/timeline.

You might even have closed and reopened Movie Maker between the copying and pasting operations.

The ability to copy a set of clips across projects, complete with effects, transitions, and titles, offers you many possibilities.

One would be to work on fine-tuning a really great 30-second standard opening that consists of a number of video clips with transitions, effects, and title overlays.

Then, for each new project, develop the body of the movie and, when finished, copy your standard opening into it. Edit the title overlay and save your movie.

Of course, you can do the same with a standard ending. Because the clips are still individual, you can easily customize the standard opening and ending for each movie and blend them into the body of the movie with smooth transitions.

Audio and title overlay clips

You can split, combine, copy, trim, and nudge audio/music clips the same way you do video clips. Advanced ways of dealing with audio clips are covered in **Chapter 7**.

Splitting, combining, and trimming don't work on title overlays. Nudging does. Use the trim handles to change the duration of the title overlay. By doing this, you can change the speed at which an animated title plays, something extremely helpful for title overlays. Titles are fully covered in **Chapter 8**.

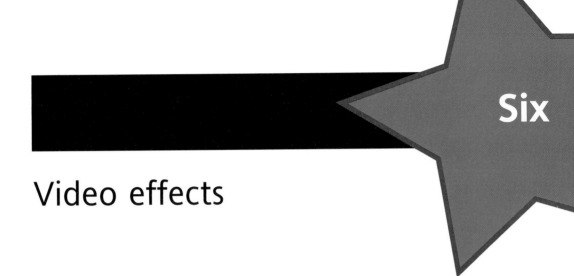

Video effects

In this chapter

A video effect is anything special that applies to some or all the frames of a clip. It may apply to part of a clip, such as fading in from black, or it may apply to the entire clip, maybe applying scratches to make it look like an old film.

In Movie Maker 2 there are 28 different standard video effects, and more can be added. You can combine them on the same clips to produce all manner of weird and wonderful effects. In this chapter, we'll take a look at how, why, and when to use video effects. This chapter will cover the following topics:

★ What video effects can achieve
★ How they are used in movies and TV
★ The effects available in Movie Maker
★ Adding video effects to clips
★ Using multiple effects on one clip
★ Adding more effects to Movie Maker

Today's camcorders have options for many effects that you can apply as you shoot your footage. It might be done optically, such as zooming, or digitally, such as changing the brightness or adding a sepia tone to the footage. With the exception of optical zoom (see **Chapter 1**), you should try not to apply these effects with your camcorder if there's an equivalent in Movie Maker you could use instead.

That's because, unlike the camcorder, nonlinear editing software gives you the ability to try them first and, crucially, remove them from footage if it hasn't turned out as planned.

Using video effects

Effects are used to enhance or correct a scene, such as brightening a dark one or dimming an overly bright one. They are also used to provide a longer-than-usual transition between segments of a movie, such as a number of clips using grayscale instead of color.

Effects for enhancement may be subtle to the point of not being noticed, such as slight changes in color. Good enhancements are perhaps best when not noticed at all. In this example, the right-hand clip has had the Brightness, Increase effect applied to it, and while it looks better, you wouldn't immediately think "that's had a video effect applied to it."

Effects can be used to add a wow! factor or a comical accent or flavor. With the Hue, Cycles Entire Color Spectrum effect applied, these phone boxes change color over the duration of the clip—perfect for that low budget sci-fi film you've been dying to make (although if you use a phone box, Doctor Who's lawyers may have a few questions for you). Whatever the reason, with Movie Maker, effects are easy to apply and try again until it looks just right.

As we said in **Chapter 4** with transitions, use effects with restraint. Let your viewers see your creativity, something that is enhanced by using appropriate effects very selectively. Experienced filmmakers don't use too many effects; they focus on the story.

A brief history

Advancements in film effects are centered on new or developing use of technology. One of the earliest special effects was zooming. The zoom lens started to be used in the late 1920s initially to illustrate the sudden change in the size of something. Much of this has to be done with a camera, but Movie Maker has Ease In and Ease Out zooming effects.

Ease In on Still Picture

Color became common in the 1930s. Occasional transitions from black and white to color were used to signify spectacle and fancy, such as in the *Wizard of Oz* in 1939. But the majority of color films in the 1930s were cartoons. Today, we take color for granted and are more impressed with occasional use of black and white or sepia-tinted clips. Movie Maker can do this easily.

Grayscale   Sepia Tone

The simplest and most commonly used effects today are the fade-in and fade-out. Fading in or out from black is probably *the* most commonly used effect, and Movie Maker can perform this easily.

You'll also be familiar with slow motion to assess a sporting event and speeding up film to watch a setting sun. By applying multiple copies of the Speed Up, Double effect, you can make a minute-long clip speed by in less than a second!

More and more effects have been developed by using technology. This has progressed to the point that it is often difficult to distinguish between reality and special effects. Movie Maker is not equipped to do a lot of what is considered to be "special effects," such as blue screening (placing actors in front of a false background), which need specially shot footage and compositing software like After Effects (www.adobe.com). Some digital video programs, like Premiere (also www.adobe.com), and Final Cut Express (www.apple.com) offer the ability to composite within the video editing environment.

Video effects in Movie Maker 2

Movie Maker includes a set of 28 video effects and allows you to install additional ones when they become available. Select the Video Effects collection, and the thumbnails or list of effects will appear in the collection contents pane.

The icons in thumbnail view attempt to show what each effect will do to your video clip. For most, this works fine, and you can see what the effect does to the standard XP landscape picture. For the ones that affect the clip over time (fades, easing, and the playing speed), there are diagrams.

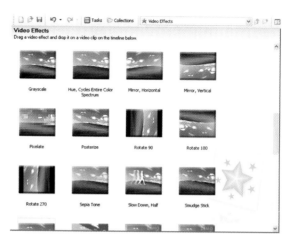

Previewing video effects

Without a doubt, the best way of getting a look at what each effect will do to your clips is to use the preview monitor.

Open the Video Effects collection and preview them by selecting one in the collection contents pane. Some effects alter every frame of the clip in the same way—Grayscale for example—and you do not need to start the preview. For other effects, press the space bar or click the Play button in the preview monitor—Movie Maker will show you how that landscape will be altered within two seconds of your chosen effect.

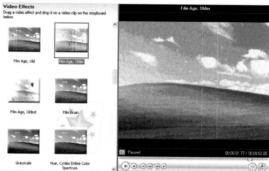

Although the preview uses a still image: the effects will be similar when applied to a video clip, it will apply the effect to each frame of the video clip in sequence.

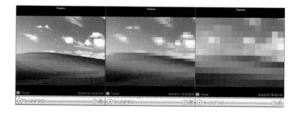

> *Previewing* Speed Up, Double, *or* Slow Down, Half *will not be of much use as they only affect video clips—playing them twice as quickly or slowly, respectively, much as you would expect.*

To preview the available effects quickly, use the details view and the up/down arrow keys to move from one effect to the next, pressing the space bar on each.

As with transitions, no matter how you resize the windows, it's not possible to see all the video effects at once—this section should help you to select the one that you want.

Still effects

Most of the video effects process the frames of your video clip in the same way as image manipulation programs filter still images. These affect every frame of a clip in exactly the same way.

Blur

Brightness, Increase

Brightness, Decrease

Grayscale

Mirror, Horizontal

Mirror, Vertical

Posterize

Rotate 90

Rotate 180

Rotate 270

Sepia Tone

Smudge Stick

Threshold

Watercolor

Film effects

These effects are intended to help give your high-quality digital video the look of having been shot on film at any time in the past hundred years! They add dust, scratches, and grain, which move across the video clip as it plays.

Film Grain

Film Age, Old

Film Age, Older

Film Age, Oldest

Fades

Four of the effects are fades in and out from black or white. These fades occur fairly quickly, in less than a second.

Fade In, From Black

Fade In, From White

Fade Out, To Black

Fade Out, To White

For a longer fade, it's easier and better to overlap a clip with a plain black or white image and by using a fade transition instead of a fade effect. See **Chapter 4** for the full instructions.

Zooms

The two zooming effects allow you to seem to get closer or further away, when you didn't move or zoom when taking the footage at all. The Ease In and Ease Out effects work well; you will usually want to apply the effect multiple times on the same clip. To zoom to or from half size, add the effect the full six times. Remember, though, that this is the same as digital zoom on your camera and will sacrifice quality.

Ease In   Ease Out

Effects over time

Two effects, Pixelate and Hue, Cycles Entire Color Spectrum, alter the image continually over the length of the clip.

 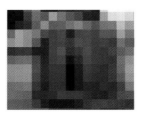  

Pixelate   Hue, Cycles Entire Color Spectrum

Faster and slower

You can double or halve the speed of a video clip with the Speed Up, Double and Slow Down, Half effects. There really isn't a way to show them in action on the printed page—the only thing you can do is to add them to a video clip and take a look; you can always remove it again.

Between these effects and the additional ones available from Microsoft and third parties, you should have no difficulties selecting effects for your movies.

Manipulating effects

Effects are applied to one clip at a time. They are easy to apply, change, and remove. The process is very similar in both storyboard and timeline views.

Adding effects in storyboard view

To use an effect in a project, it's easiest to start in the storyboard view of your project with the Video Effects collection selected. You will probably be doing the review and selection of effects late in the project development, after most of the clips are on the storyboard and transitions have been applied.

> *The speed up and slow down effects will change the duration of the clips, so you might want to apply those particular effects before audio narrative or music tracks are finalized.*

Scroll through the project clips, preview the available effects, and drag selected effects to the clips. The star box at the lower left corner of the clip box will change from gray to blue when the first effect is added. If you add additional effects to the same clip, the box will show a double star.

Kynoch Air Shot

Kynoch Air Shot

Hover over the star with your mouse cursor and the tooltip will list the effects currently applied to the clip.

You can add as many as six effects to each clip. It can be six different effects, the same effect added six times, or any combination of one or more effects.

Adding effects in timeline view

In timeline view, you can also drag effects from the collection contents pane onto your clips.

Select your effect and drag it onto the clip in the timeline.

Clips that have an effect applied to them will show a blue star; clips with more than one effect show the doubled star.

You cannot see which effects are applied in timeline view by hovering your pointer over the stars; no tooltip appears. This is one reason for favoring the storyboard view when adding effects.

The Video Effects box

You can only drag and drop effects one at a time onto a clip when using the Video Effects content pane, but you can right-click any clip on the storyboard/timeline and choose Video Effects.

The box contains two lists: Available effects, which is the list of video effects installed on your system, and Displayed effects, which is a list of effects currently applied to your clip.

The Video Effects dialog box allows you to add or remove effects easily and change the sequence that they are applied.

To add an effect with this box, select it in the Available effects list and click Add.

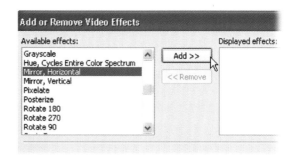

It will be added to the Displayed effects list, above the selected effect if there are already effects in the list.

To remove an effect, select it in the Displayed effects list and click on Remove.

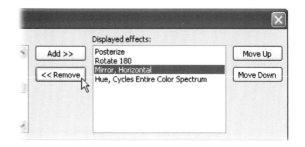

You can add up to six effects onto any one clip; some combinations will be very different if the sequence you apply them in is changed. Others will not noticeably change.

You can change the sequence by which effects are applied by using the Move Up and Move Down buttons on the right side of the Video Effects dialog box.

Trying different options is best when selecting the sequence.

Multiple effects

The end result of using multiple effects will sometimes be additive, and sometimes they will cancel each other out.

Three copies of the Rotate 90 effect is the same as adding the Rotate 270 effect once.

Four copies of Rotate 90 would be the same as not applying any effects at all.

The effects are applied to the clip, from the list, in top-down order. This means that the effects lower down will be applied over the top of the clips further up the list.

Rotate 270   Rotate 90
                     Rotate 90
                     Rotate 90

If the effect lower down overwrites the effect of the first, as is the case here with the Sepia Tone and Grayscale effects, then only the one lower down the list will have any effect.

If you use three Ease Ins followed by three Ease Outs on the same clip, they will cancel each other, not ease in for the first half of the clip and out for the second half.

Grayscale, Sepia Tone   Sepia Tone, Grayscale

You would have to use the clip twice (if a still picture) or split a video clip and apply the Ease Ins to the first one and the Ease Outs to the second.

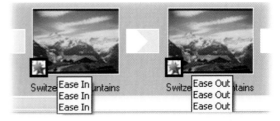

Try this for yourself or watch this pair of effects at www.friendsofed.com.

If you split a clip, all effects applied to it are automatically applied to each of the two new clips. If you combine clips with different effects on them, the effects on the first clip will apply to the combined clip.

Experimenting is probably the best course of action when it comes to combining and sequencing effects; seemingly unconnected effects will alter the clips when applied in different orders.

Changing and removing effects

To change an effect, right-click the clip in the storyboard or timeline view and choose Video Effects from the menu to bring up the dialog box to add or remove effects.

Blur, Watercolor   Watercolor, Blur

To remove all effects from a clip, it's easiest in the storyboard view. Select the transition star on the clip and press DELETE, or right-click on the star and choose Delete Effects.

In the timeline view, you can see the star but you can't select it. If you try to select it and delete the effects, you'll delete the clip instead.

Using effects creatively

Here are a couple of examples of using Movie Maker's effects in real projects.

Easing in

Ease in on a still picture to better integrate it into a movie. If you apply the effect a number of times, use a high resolution picture. Have the subject fairly close to the center of the image, or crop the picture first to get the subject where you want. The high resolution image will have to provide enough pixels for the portion zoomed into to retain quality.

For a saved movie of 640x480 pixels, use a still image or video clip of at least twice its size (1280x960) if applying the Ease In effect six times.

Here, the original picture was 2160x1440 pixels from a 3.1-megapixel still camera. The duration on the timeline was expanded to 20 seconds, and the Ease In effect was applied six times.

The clip in the saved movie looked better than the clip in the preview in Movie Maker, so these screen shots show the first and last frames of the finished movie as it looked in the Windows Media Player.

Ease In—Start   Ease Out—Start

Slow motion

Another example is the slow motion effect. Here we've applied it to watch a skiing mishap, enjoying it after the fact because the individual was not hurt.

In this scene, the Slow Down, Half effect was applied twice to get it to an appropriate playback speed.

Because the incident was unplanned and happened quickly, the person taking the video didn't have time to zoom in, so the Ease In effect is used four times to better concentrate on the subject.

This used all six of the allotted effects.

To apply additional ones, you could save the single clip with effects applied to it as a movie to an AVI file (for more information on saving movies, see **Chapter 9**) and then import it to Movie Maker as a new clip ready for up to six more effects.

You could apply additional effects, perhaps brightening the scene or possibly even zooming in closer. This saving and re-importing trick is something that we'll use again in **Chapters 7** and **8**.

Keeping it professional

There are some things to avoid when using effects, if you want to give your movies that professional sheen.

Overusing the effects you like most will make the video seem amateurish right from the start. Misusing an effect can be worse than not using one at all. And using an effect on a clip that doesn't need one, or without a purpose in mind, will detract from the scene or even from the whole movie.

You can easily get so enamored with a particular effect that you might take every opportunity to use it. If you love the slow motion effect, you might apply it to everything moving at fast speed or even normal speed.

As you choose each effect, ask yourself if you are using it to show off the effect or to enhance the clip or the flow of the video as it will be viewed by your audience. If you opt for more than one slow-speed clip in a 15-minute skiing movie, it might be too much. Additional slow-motion scenes would downplay the use of the effect on the clip that is most enhanced by it. Mix the location and frequency when applying effects.

As noted in **Chapter 4** on transitions, a good place to practice using effects and transitions is on introductory and closing clips. You can mix video clips, still pictures, sound, special video and transition effects, text, etc. The mixture can be as artistic or wild as you want, without taking away from the main body of the movie.

Extra effects

The Microsoft Plus! Digital Media Edition, available for purchase from Microsoft, has 25 additional effects. In Movie Maker, choose Help > Windows Movie Maker on the Web to go to Microsoft's web site for Movie Maker information. The site includes links to Microsoft and third-party software.

Pixelan, one third-party developer, has released an effects package for Movie Maker 2. It is available in a fully functional demo in addition to the full release (the demo embeds a big X along with the effect, which is not present when you purchase the software). There are 25 effects in the Pixelan package, most of them changes to colors—tones, tints, saturation. If you have downloaded the Pixelan extra transitions, the effects will probably have been installed with them.

After installing additional effects and restarting Movie Maker, the added effects will show up in the Video Effects collection along with the original ones. The thumbnails provide brief previews, and you can see the effects in the preview monitor. The Pixelan thumbnails are similar to those of Movie Maker but say Format text on them.

Like Photoshop and Premiere filters, video effects will eventually be customized by end users. Movie Maker opens the door to third parties providing effects. Look out for many more of them to supplement those now available.

Be aware that Movie Maker uses more computer memory when additional effects are added. The extra memory used when the Pixelan effects package is installed is about 7MB. If you have lots of RAM, this is a modest amount. If you are trying to minimize memory demands, you can remove the package out of the `Movie Maker Shared` subfolder after installing it, and then copy it back for sessions that use it.

Audio editing

In this chapter

Although for the most part, you can edit and assemble sounds and music in your movie projects in much the same way that you can with video clips, there are many complexities added by the ability to mix audio across tracks.

You are able to decide the volume levels of each clip individually, as well as the relative levels of the Audio/Music track and Audio for Video track. Movie Maker can even be used to record your own audio track. This chapter will explain all the options you have and decisions you have to make when editing the audio of your movie projects. This chapter will cover the following topics:

★ Adding sound to the Audio/Music track
★ Adjusting audio levels
★ Adjusting the volume of individual clips
★ Fading in and out
★ Adding commentary to your movie
★ Correcting sound glitches
★ Editing video to synchronize with sound
★ Creating audio transitions to enhance your movies

Sound in Movie Maker 2

Sound, like almost everything in Movie Maker, is handled as clips. You can import sound files into your collections just as you can import still pictures or video files, and you can also use Movie Maker to record sound from your computer's microphone.

The most important thing to remember about sound clips is that the final audio of your finished movie is the result of Movie Maker **combining** and **mixing** the audio in the two separate audio tracks. Most of the sections in this chapter involve in some way manipulating the audio levels of the Audio/Music track and Audio for Video track, as well as the clips themselves.

When working with sound, it is always best to use the timeline view, with the Video track expanded, so you can see and manipulate any of the sound in your movie project easily.

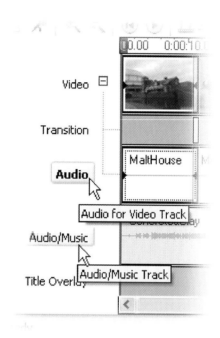

Adding clips to the Audio/Music track

You can add any sound clip from your collections, to the Audio/Music track, this includes video clips as well as the audio clips that are represented by a note as a thumbnail. The process of importing audio clips into your collections is covered in **Chapter 3**.

The Audio/Music track only contributes sound to the final movie, so video clips placed here will not be seen—only heard. This can be useful, however, as we'll see when we get into using sound in more advanced ways.

Collection: The International
Drag a clip and drop it on the timeline below.

Joan Of Arc Was In The
Go-Gos

Justine

1. To add a clip to the Audio/Music track, simply select it in the collection contents pane and drag it into position on the timeline.

2. Clips in the Audio/Music track can be positioned anywhere along the timeline. If you drop a clip on a period where there isn't a clip in the timeline, wherever you drop the clip will be its starting point. If there isn't enough room for the full length of the clip, subsequent clips in the track are pushed back.

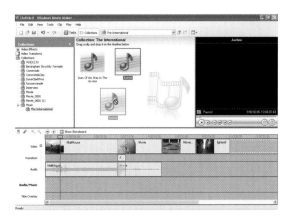

3. If you drop a clip on top of one already in the Audio/Music track, then the blue I symbol will appear, indicating whether the new clip will be placed before or after the one already in the timeline.

The clips appear in the timeline with a waveform to indicate their volume.

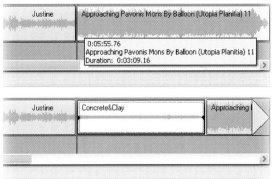

Audio levels and volume

The audio levels in Movie Maker control just how much of each of the audio tracks will be heard in the finished (or previewed) movie. To bring up the adjustment slider in its window, click on the Set Audio Levels icon above and to the left of the timeline.

You can only adjust this slider for the project as a whole. All the way left will silence the Audio/Music track in favor of the sound that is attached to the video clips; adjusting it to the right will silence the video sound.

Unless you know exactly how the audio should sound in your final movie, only the sound in the Audio/Music track for a music video for example, it is best to experiment with this level after you've finished editing your movie, adjusting it for the best overall result.

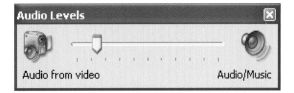

During editing, you are best off leaving it in the center somewhere, so you don't miss any mistakes in the sound that may end up in your finished movie.

Clip volume

While in a collection, all clips have a default volume to allow you to preview them easily, but you have more control than just the Audio Levels setting of the volume of clips in your movie. Each can be set separately in the timeline—this applies to both audio clips in the Audio/Music track and to the sound attached to a video clip.

1. To adjust the volume of a clip, first select it in the timeline.

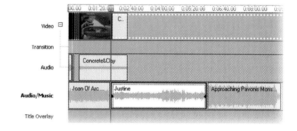

2. Then open the Audio Clip Volume dialog box by right-clicking and selecting Volume...or choosing Clip > Audio > Volume.... The keyboard shortcut is CTRL+U.

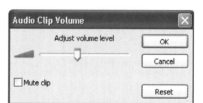

3. You can adjust the volume of the clip from silent to the maximum level of your computer and all points in between. Simply click and drag the slider.

4. By default, each clip is set at half volume, which you can return to at anytime by clicking on the Reset button.

5. To **mute** (silence) the clip, you can select the box that says Mute clip. It will check itself if you slide all the way to the left.

6. There's no way of telling exactly how loud the clips will sound with the dialog box open. You simply have to click OK and then preview the movie, returning to the dialog box if the sound is not quite to your liking.

When you have adjusted the volume of a clip, the change is reflected by the waveform graph in the timeline. As you can see in these diagrams, the higher the volume, the larger the **waveform** is.

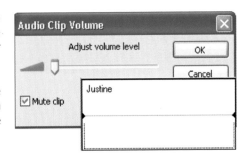

If the peaks of the audio are above the level that the computer can deal with, reflected by the waveform graph hitting the top and bottom of the box, then the sound may be muffled through your speakers.

> *When adjusting the volume, check the waveform —if the sound's peaks are off the scale, lower the volume for clear reproduction.*

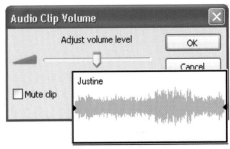

The volume set in this dialog box is relative to the volume at which the clip was recorded. It might not be possible to make a very quiet clip as loud as you want, while you may not have as fine control over an especially loud clip as you would like.

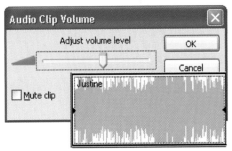

Audio effects

There are three audio effects that Movie Maker can perform automatically: muting the clip, fading in, and fading out.

Muting clips

As well as setting the volume of a clip to zero in the Audio Clip Volume dialog box, you can quickly silence an entire clip by right-clicking on it and selecting Mute (or selecting the clip and Clip > Audio > Mute).

This can be useful when you need to silence a whole lot of video clips so that the sound in the Audio/Music track can be heard. You can simply select multiple clips in the Audio for Video track and mute them.

Fading in and out

If you select a clip and select Fade In (either by right-clicking or from the menu Clip > Audio > Fade In), the audio clip will fade in from silence when played.

Similarly, if you select a clip and select Fade Out (either by right-clicking or from the menu Clip > Audio > Fade Out), the audio clip will fade out to silence when it has finished playing.

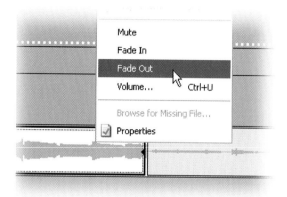

Selecting the same options again will turn the fades off.

You have no control over how quickly the fades happen. They are over in no time at all, even fast enough not to be shown by the waveform. Fades are most useful to soften transitions between loud and quiet sound clips next to each other in the timeline—when there isn't enough spare room for a clip for a soft transition.

Narrating your movie

You can add a running commentary or a narration to your movie, watching it as it goes along, and Movie Maker will record it for you and place it directly in the timeline.

Once your movie is all set up in the Video and Title Overlay tracks, you can start to record directly into your computer's microphone.

> *The narration clip automatically goes onto the* Audio/Music *track of the timeline. This means that you can't have both narration and background music in the same part of the timeline.*

1. The narration will start to be recorded from the current position of the playhead—so make sure it's where you want it to start.

You can only begin narration from a place on the timeline that doesn't already have an clip in the Audio/Music track. (We'll cover mixing more than one audio track after this example.)

2. From the menu, select Tools > Narrate Timeline, or click on the Narrate Timeline icon above the storyboard/timeline. This will toggle you to timeline view if you are not there and open the Narrate Timeline pane.

3. Select Show more options in the Narrate Timeline pane to see additional options. You will need to do this to set your input source if it isn't selected as default.

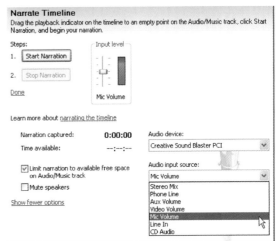

4. To select your input source, you need to make sure that you have the correct settings for these options:

   ★ Audio device: this should be the computer's capture sound device. This will usually be the sound card, and you may only have one option here.

   ★ Audio input source: choose your input source from the drop-down list. The list of options here will depend on the hardware connected to your computer, but Mic Volume or Microphone should be available—select this to record from a microphone connected to your computer.

The other extra information on show follows:

   ★ Narration captured: as you record your commentary, the length will show here in the format Hours:Minutes:Seconds.

   ★ Time available: the display here shows the amount of time between the current position of the playhead on the timeline and the start of the next clip on the Audio/Music track.

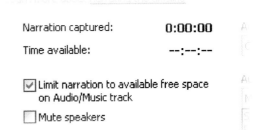

If you already have clips on the Audio/Music track, you cannot narrate the entire length of your movie. If you continue to talk over the background music track, the music clip will be pushed along the timeline when your narration clip is inserted.

The option to Limit narration to available free space on Audio/Music track helps you to avoid this. When selected, the narration will automatically stop when the preview reaches the start of the next clip on the Audio/Music track.

The Mute speakers option stops sound coming from the computer speakers as you narrate—check this to prevent feedback. Unless you are using an input source that you can't hear otherwise, it's best to select this option. You probably wouldn't want to mute your speakers if you were getting audio from another device (say a MiniDisc player into the line-in socket) rather than a live microphone.

5. Test your input level with the audio meter either by speaking into your microphone or by starting input from your source.

The input level meter rises and falls much like a graphic equalizer on a stereo system.

If your audio doesn't peak high enough, you won't be able to hear it in the finished movie. If it peaks in the red too often, you will get muffled, poor-quality sound.

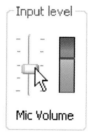

6. Adjust the slider, rather than your input's volume level. Set it so it goes routinely into the upper end but not into the red area.

7. When you've set everything up and are ready to start the narration, click the Start Narration button. If the microphone input is selected, talk into it; otherwise, start whatever source you're using.

You now get to watch a preview of your movie and talk along with it. You've probably seen the movie project all the way through a couple of times by now, but you will no doubt trip up over your words or forget what you were going to say. It will help immensely if you work out a basic script, especially if you are intending to narrate the entire length of a long movie.

Don't forget that you can stop and start the narration as many times as you want and also remove or edit the sound clips that are created, just as you can any other. If you make just a small mistake, don't worry and keep going—it'll probably be possible to correct that later.

Try to minimize the eventuality of having to do such repair jobs, though, by having a practice run or two first.

You should also make sure that there's no background noise that will be heard on your narration. Record your narration in the quietest situation possible—wait until the rest of the family is out!

8. When you've finished this part of the narration (or the whole movie, if you've been brave!), click the Stop Narration button. A Save Windows Media File dialog box will open, letting you name the narration file and the folder to store it in. It won't let you overwrite an existing narration file.

9. The saved file will be WMA and the default location is My Documents\My Videos\ Narration folder. You can change the location when you name the file, but if you move or delete the file at a later date, it will be missing from your movie project.

Mixing narration and background music

It is unfortunate that you cannot mix narration with background music easily in Movie Maker, as most professional documentaries or narrated sections in films do. You can, however, mix it yourself with a little extra effort.

1. Create a movie first, using video clips, titles, and music clips for the background. Save it to your hard drive at as high a quality as you have space for (see **Chapter 9** for full details on saving movies).

2. Then, import the saved movie to a new collection, remembering not to allow Movie Maker to create clips automatically.

3. Drag the clip onto a new timeline in the Video track and add narration, remembering to mute the speakers as you do so.

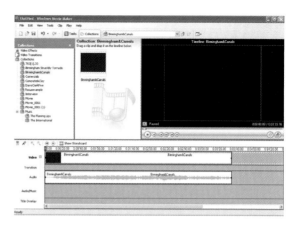

Because the imported movie is now one large video clip (which contains all the tracks that were in its movie project timeline), it will sit only on the Video track—leaving the Audio/Music track free for narration.

4. When you've narrated your movie, you can save it again for whatever output type it is intended. First, adjust the audio levels until you're happy with the mix.

You could repeat this process as many times as you want to overlay many different audio/music/ narration clips.

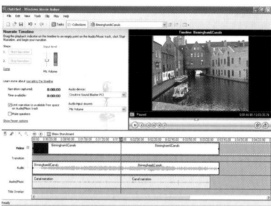

Correcting sound mistakes

It's possible, with some judicious splitting of sound clips, to correct harshness and certain mistakes in the sound that you've recorded and imported for your movie projects. You will need to use different methods, depending on whether the sound is part of a video clip or not.

Removing noise from clips in the Audio/Music track

You may have a clip in the Audio/Music track that has a section of unwanted noise: a door closing while you were narrating your movie, for example, or a section of narration where you stumbled over a word. You can rid yourself of this, within reason, by splitting your clip and deleting the bad section.

If you'd like to follow along with this exercise, compressed versions of the source files are available to download from www.friendsofed.com. You can simply practice the techniques on your own clips—but if you'd like to, import the files into a Movie Maker collection and drag the video clip `Birmingham&Canals` to the Video track and the audio clip to the start of the Audio/Music track.

1. First, listen to your Audio/Music track closely. It'll help to adjust the audio levels to silence the sound coming from the Video track to find the section of the clip that has the problem.

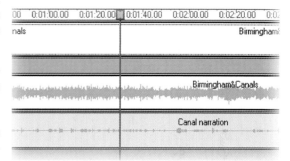

In this case, there is the sound of the narrator breathing loudly onto the microphone at around the 1:30 mark.

2. Zoom in as close as possible to the point on the timeline where the unwanted sound appears. Play that section of your clip over and over, watching the waveform moving past the playhead. Try to identify the part of the wave that is the unwanted sound.

It may help to do this if you increase the volume of the clip so that the waveform is more noticeable. You can adjust the level again after you've finished.

The breath actually started at 1:32 and is represented by the highlighted part of the waveform:

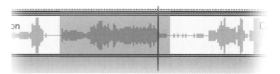

3. When you're sure that you've identified the unwanted sound, you need to move the playhead to the start of the waveform that represents it, making sure that you position it on a period of quiet (a flat line).

4. Select the clip containing the bad section and click on the Split Clip button in the preview monitor. The clip will split at that point.

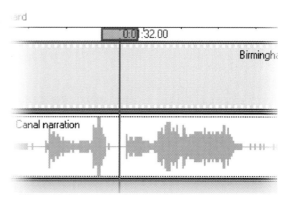

5. Move the playhead to the end of the unwanted part of the wave, again making sure that the position you select is as near to silence as possible. Select the clip and click on the Split Clip button again.

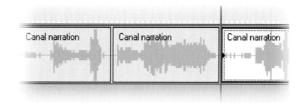

You now have three clips on the timeline; the middle one should contain nothing but the unwanted sound.

6. Select the central clip and press DELETE—removing it from the timeline.

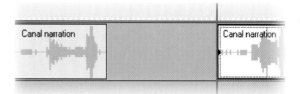

Preview this part of your movie to make sure that it sounds right; if not, you may notice that the audio clips at the wrong place. Press CTRL+N to put the deleted clip back, combine the three clips, and try again.

If the bad section didn't contain any words (or other sounds) that are essential to your soundtrack, then you've finished and can move on to something else in your movie.

If the noise happens at the same time as part of your narration, then you can still delete that part, but you'll have to record some new narration to fit in the gap.

Recording pick-ups

If you stumble over your words or there is a background noise at the same time as you were narrating the timeline and it's not possible simply to remove that section of the clip, it can still be fixed.

Recording parts of a speech or narration again to correct mistakes is called recording a **pick-up**—and don't worry, it's not looked on with scorn; the big Hollywood stars do it all the time.

1. First, identify the part of the waveform that is the problem, as above. You may need to select more of the clip than the problem—it will sound unnatural if we attempt to re-record part of a section that doesn't have a natural pause.

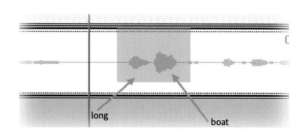

Here the narrator has got his lines wrong, referring to the boat on the canal as a longboat (which is what Viking ships are called) instead of a narrow boat. The highlighted section all needs replacing, but only the first peak "long" is actually wrong—the second peak "boat" will be replaced so that the finished version sounds more realistic.

2. Decide on the incorrect part of the clip and split the clip twice as we did previously, leaving the part to be removed as a separate clip.

3. Delete the central clip, and preview the timeline. You'll hear the gap that removing that section has created.

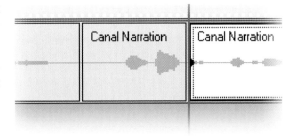

4. Move the playhead to the start of the gap, and open the Narrate Timeline pane. Test your input levels as we need to re-record our bad section.

5. Check the Limit narration... box to stop moving the clip after the gap, and re-record the words. Click Start Narration to start, and Movie Maker itself will stop you when the gap is filled.

The difficult part here is making your voice sound the same as it did when you originally recorded the narration (doubly so if you are using the downloaded file, as it wasn't you!). Don't worry; even professional voice-over actors have trouble with this. You can always delete the newly recorded clip and try again.

6. Save the new clip and it will be imported into your timeline. Hopefully the replacement words will fit perfectly; if not, you may have to practice a little more.

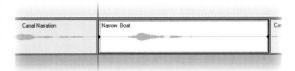

Hiding bad sound on a video clip

You cannot cut out or replace bad sound that is attached to a video clip in the same way; cutting out part of the sound will also cut out the corresponding part of the video. In a Hollywood production, they would probably reshoot the whole scene as recording new versions of location soundtracks is very difficult. Often with home movies, that's not possible—whatever our budget—so if a part of an otherwise good clip is ruined by a unwanted sound, we have to do our best mask it.

1. Zoom in on the offending part of your sound in the Audio for Video track of the timeline, and identify the part of the waveform that is a problem.

In this clip (available for download), the noise of a shoe scraping on the pavement at around 06:40 jars with the rest of the hustle and bustle of the city street scene.

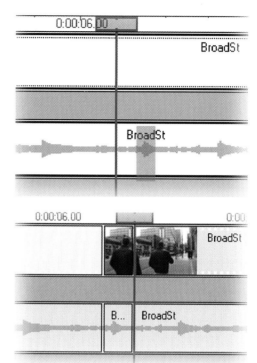

2. Move the playhead to just before the bad sound, again when the waveform is as close to silent as possible, and split the clip.

3. Split the clip again after the offending sound, keeping the three clips in the Video track.

As you can see, splitting the audio here also splits the video into three clips. Deleting the central one will leave a nasty jump in the film. Try it if you like—then Undo (CTRL+Z) afterward.

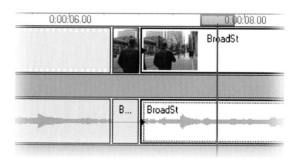

4. Although we can't remove the clip, we can silence it. Right-click on the central clip and choose Mute from the menu.

> *In clips without much background noise and with one offending jolt of sound, this may be enough. In this instance, the sudden silence is as jarring as the noise was to start with.*

5. Open the Audio Clip Volume dialog box for the clip (CTRL+U), and clear Mute. Drag the volume of the clip down, but not all the way—around a quarter of full volume is a good level to choose.

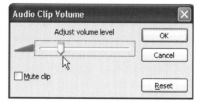

6. Click OK and test your clip. If the bad sound is still too loud, adjust the clip volume of the central clip down a little more. If that clip is too quiet, raise it a little.

By selectively adjusting the volume of parts of the soundtrack in this way, you can save video clips that would have been potentially ruined. If you eventually add a piece of background music to the clip, your audience may not notice anything wrong at all.

Replacing bad sound on a video clip

The other way to fix a sound problem with a video clip is to replace the soundtrack completely with sounds that could have been heard at the same time. Often filmmakers will record sound at a location, just to record background noise. These pieces of audio, called **wildtracks**, are used to replace poor quality sound in otherwise good takes.

Although it will not work with dialog, you can replace background noise in a video clip with some recorded at a different time or in a different location.

The two clips used for demonstration here are available for download from www.friendsofed.com.

1. Import your clips, both the one with poor audio and the wildtrack, into Movie Maker.

Collection: Pan
Drag a clip and drop it on the timeline below.

Pan   Squirrels

2. Start a new project and drag your clip with poor sound onto the timeline in the Video track. Right-click on the clip and choose Mute.

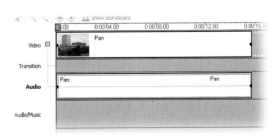

The Pan clip (of the view from a bridge) is spoiled by the sound of high wind and footsteps. The wildtrack clip comes from some footage of squirrels feeding from a bird table. There is little sound in the clip, just a soft breeze and occasional bird calls.

3. Now drag your clip that you're using as a wildtrack into the timeline on the Audio/Music track.

4. If the wildtrack clip is not as long as your clip, drag multiple copies into the Audio/Music track until it covers more of the timeline than the video clip.

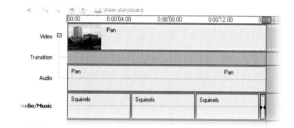

5. Trim the right edge of the last clip in the Audio/Music track so it finishes at the same point as the clip in the Video track.

6. Save the movie to your hard drive at as high a quality as you have space for (see **Chapter 9** for full details on saving movies).

7. Then import the saved movie back into Movie Maker for use as a normal video clip.

Editing video to music

Often, you will want to use a piece of music as the main point of your video and base the way the video clips are put together on the pace of the song. This is the basis for the way most music videos and sports clip highlights are made, and it's an ideal way to pace short home movies.

This example uses one of the sample pieces of music that comes with Windows XP: Beethoven's Symphony No. 9. You can use any you like, but the peaks and valleys in this recording make it easy to demonstrate the technique.

1. Choose the music that you'd like to use and import it into a Movie Maker collection. Start a new project and drag it to the start of the Audio/Music track in the timeline.

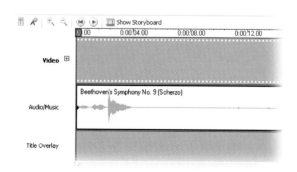

2. Take a good look at the waveform that displays the volume of the clip; it gives you a good indication of the flow of the music. Sharp peaks are musical "stings," while long passages of the piece that are musically similar will be around the same height in the waveform graph.

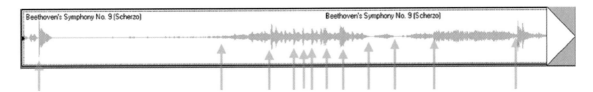

The transitions between sections, or the peaks in the waveform, are ideal places to cut from one scene or image to another. Think about the video clips that you've got to edit to the music. If you've got long sections of video, then they are going to be best placed where there are no "stings."

> *The more beats there are in the piece of music, the more, and shorter, clips you're going to need to edit into the finished movie.*

3. Start at the beginning and add what you've decided will be your opening shot to the Video track. Trim it from the right so that it finishes just after the first major peak.

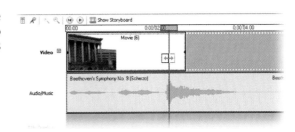

4. Drag your next video clip into the timeline and then preview the start of the movie. Watch and listen as the cut between scenes happens at the same time as the musical transition. This is the main principle of editing video clips to music.

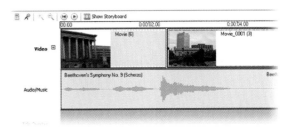

5. Continue to trim and add more clips, changing scenes where the music indicates to you that you should.

If you have a very long stretch of similar music, consider joining two clips with a smooth transition rather than a sharp cut. This will allow you to keep your audience interested in the visuals without distracting them from the music track. Watch how the professionals assemble their clips to music—it can be done with Movie Maker.

Audio transitions

In this book, we've a whole chapter dedicated to transitions between video clips (that's **Chapter 4**, if you haven't seen it) and the many special effects you can apply to them. Audio transitions are different in that, apart from the simple fade across, it's up to you to make them yourself.

You can overlap audio clips in the Audio/Music track in the same way that you can overlay video clips in the video track (as is discussed in **Chapter 3**). This overlap causes the second clip to fade in over the top of the first.

Overlapping video clips for a fade will also overlap and fade the sound in the Audio for Video track.

The fade transitions in Movie Maker are best used with a video fade to or from a flat color.

Advanced audio transitions

When you assess a project to determine when to add a video transition, think about adding audio transitions also. Sound and video should not be edited as seperate entities.

Audio, when started earlier than the video of a clip, can raise the viewer's expectation of an upcoming scene. Likewise, when audio is carried over a bit into a following scene, it can reinforce and carry forth the message that the first clip is expressing, binding the two clips much closer together. Such audio transitions can be very effective in achieving a finely polished video.

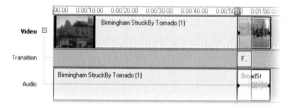

These two audio transitions can add a lot to the professionalism of your videos, but they are not as easy to implement as simple fades. A transition where the sound of a clip continues after the video of the next clip starts is called an **L-Cut**.

If the sound of the upcoming clip starts a little before the current video clip ends, it's a **J-Cut**. Think about the shape of the letters L and J, with the audio clip on the timeline under the video clip, and you'll see where the terms come from.

An audio J-cut or L-cut will either start the sound of the next clip before the current clip ends or carry the current clip's audio somewhat into the following clip.

Creating an L-cut

Sound should flow across scenes to be most effective. Editors often carry the sound of someone speaking across the cut and into the next clip, which is an L-cut. The editor uses the last few words of the person speaking from the first clip over the start of the following reaction clip (the person hearing it).

Here's an example of an L-cut. This video clip in the timeline of this project is of a man talking about a goal he's seen his favorite soccer team score. It has quite good audio but is dark and not very interesting to look at. So we'll use an L-cut to cut away to a picture of one of the players. Both the video clip and the picture are available for download from the downloads section on www.friendsofED.com.

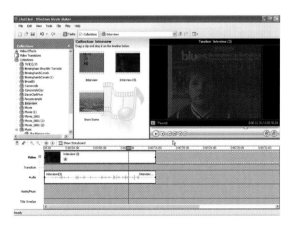

1. First drag the audio track from the Audio for Video track of the Video and drop it into the Audio/Music track.

2. The clip in the Video track disappears when you do this, so drag another copy of the video clip into the Video track on the timeline.

3. Then cut the video where the talking head starts to get a bit boring, and delete the part you don't want.

It's easy to see now where the term L-cut comes from.

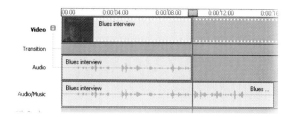

4. Mute the audio clip that remains on the Audio for Video track so that only the copy on the Audio/Music track is heard. This is to ensure that, even if you haven't lined up the audio on the Audio/Music track with the video clip exactly, the sound will seem to be in sync.

5. Add the still picture or second video clip to the Video track. If you are using a video clip with sound, make sure that it will not interfere with the audio of the L-cutting clip. You may have to mute its audio component in the Audio for Video track, or at least reduce its volume.

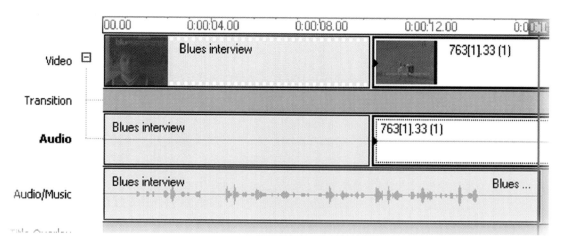

You can see that the original audio of the clip now overlaps the second clip, providing the audio L-cut.

Creating a J-cut

Let's try a J-cut with the same materials. The difference here is that you delete the first part of the clip, causing problems with syncing the audio track.

Start with the clip to have its audio J-cut in the Video track of a new project.

1. Again, drag the audio track from the Audio for Video track of the Video and drop it into the Audio/Music track.

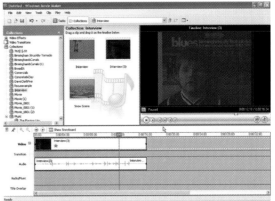

2. Drag another copy of the video clip into the Video track on the timeline.

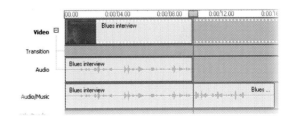

3. Choose where you would like to start to see the picture of the main clip, split the clip (in the Video track) into three, and delete the first half. The clip in the Video track will shift off to the left, making it out of sync with the audio in the Audio/Music track.

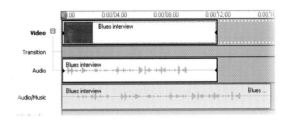

4. Insert the picture or other clip to the left of the video clip in the timeline—the video clip will move back right, but not necessarily the right amount.

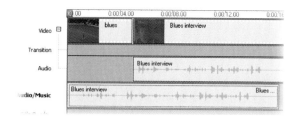

5. Either trim the first clip in the timeline or drag the second clip across (creating a transition) until the audio of the J-cut clip aligns in the Audio/Music and Audio for Video tracks. You can test this by previewing the timeline and listening for weird audio echoes. When there are none, the clips are in sync.

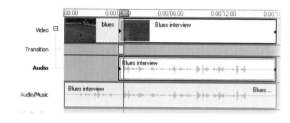

6. Mute the version in the Audio for Video track and your J-cut is complete.

Use the Audio/Music track for making L- and J-cuts, and when you finish editing the movie, save it (at the highest quality possible) and then re-import it as a new single uncut clip.

Place it on the timeline in a new project and add the background music. Although it's a two-pass process, you can easily add sophisticated audio transitions while still having the background music.

Titles and credits

In this chapter

Once you've built your movie from clips in the storyboard and timeline, added effects to them and transitions between them, it's almost time for the premiere. The final ingredients added to most films are the titles and credits, and Movie Maker 2 can create a wealth of text effects.

It's simple, once you know how, to use the wizards to create titles and credits—and, with a bit of creativity, you can duplicate nearly anything you see on TV. In this chapter, we'll go through the process of creating titles and credits. This chapter will cover the following:

★ Adding titles, credits, and captions before, after, and during your movie
★ Choosing the right style for your project
★ Customizing titles by changing fonts, colors, and sizes
★ Layering text over video and still pictures
★ Adding special effects to titles

What can you do with titles?

Titles and credits are just text on screen; **captions** might be a better word. Although traditionally television programs and films have a title sequence at the start and a scrolling list of credits at the end, you can use the Titles and Credits wizard to add text at any point in your movie project.

This could be a caption like those in documentaries when introducing a new person, sports results, or even subtitles. Whenever or wherever in your movie you'd like to add text, you can—even putting title styles together with video effects or overlaying them with other clips in cunning ways to create great-looking captions.

Creating and adding titles/credits

All the different types of titles and credits are created with the same wizard and then added to your movie at the point you specify. You can start the wizard and create the titles or credits at any time in your movie editing process. If you like, you can create your end credits first and build the movie by inserting clips in front of it, or you may choose to start with your opening titles.

Most people find it easier to leave adding the text to the end of the movie-making process, it's easy to experiment with different titling styles and animations, and you'll want to see how each looks in the context of your finished project.

> *If you want your titles to appear over the top of a video clip or still image rather than on a plain background, you need to select that clip in the storyboard/timeline before starting the process.*

1. Choose and select your clip if needed and then start the Titles and Credits wizard by choosing Tools > Titles and Credits… or clicking on Make titles or credits from the movie tasks pane.

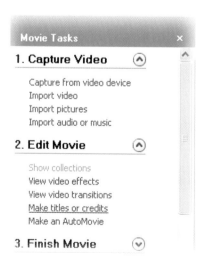

The wizard will create a new clip and add it straight into the timeline. Completed titles and credits do not appear in a collection but are edited and saved as part of your project file.

Choosing where to add a title

The full list of options to position your title follows:

★ Add title at the beginning of the movie—creates the title clip at the far left of the timeline, moving everything in the Video track (including transitions) back. Any music or narration in the Audio track stays where it is.

★ Add title before the selected clip in the timeline—creates a title clip in the Video track, in the middle of your movie, moving clips later in your project back. Sound clips in the Audio track do not move.

★ Add title on the selected clip—the title will appear in the Title Overlay track to be found at the bottom of the timeline. It does not move any other clips but for its duration will appear overlaid on the clip(s) in the Video track.

★ Add title after the selected clip on the timeline—adds the title into the Video track to the right of the selected clip, pushing subsequent clips back. Again, sound in the Audio track is unaffected.

★ Add credits at the end of the movie—adds the clip at the end of movie project into the Video track. As it appears at the end of the movie it doesn't affect the position of any other track.

2. Make your choice and click on the option.

Adding text, choosing an animation style

Movie Maker shows you a preview of how the finished title will look as you create it. Any alterations you make in the title, text, fonts, sizes, colors, or animations will be refelected in the preview monitor.

3. But of course, you won't see anything unless you type some text. Type anything you like into the boxes on screen. Pressing TAB will move you to the next box.

Depending on the animation that you choose, Movie Maker shows more or fewer text boxes (and allows you to fit varying amounts of characters into them). Credit styles allow you to add more lines of boxes by pressing ENTER when you reach the last one.

If you switch between animation styles, you may not see everything you've entered. But don't worry, it will still remember all of it and, if you switch back, it will reappear.

4. To change between animation styles, click on Change the title animation. There is now a scrolling list of title animation styles, where the text box was.

The titles are divided into three categories: Titles, One Line, Titles, Two Lines, and Credits. They all have a name and a description of what happens to the text on screen.

5. Choose an animation and select it. The preview window will show you how it looks with your text.

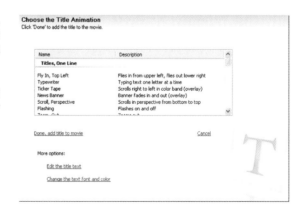

Choosing fonts, sizes, and colors

You can alter the look of your titles still further.

6. Click on the option to Change the text font and color.

The window will show all the options for modifying the text. A lot of the buttons will be familiar to you from word processors and other computer programs, and they will all work in much the same way.

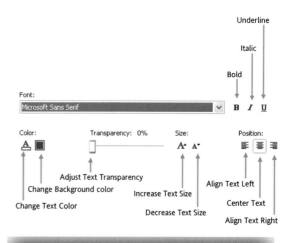

7. Select a font from the Font: drop-down menu. You'll see a list of all fonts currently installed on your computer. You can select any one that you please, and that will be used for your title.

Without knowing it, people associate different type styles with different types of films, and making the wrong decision here will confuse your audience.

The first font here, called Westminster, is definitely space-age; it just doesn't look right for a cowboy movie. Changing to another font, in this case Playbill, makes all the difference.

> *Some fonts work well for video titling, some don't. More ornate fonts are lost against background images. A font that is difficult to read is not a good choice for a caption that is not on screen for long. You should choose your font carefully.*

8. You can choose to have your text **bold**, *italic*, <u>underlined</u>, or a combination of the three. Unlike a word processor, however, Movie Maker applies the style to the whole title. You cannot select individual words.

9. To change the size of the text on screen, use the buttons under the word Size, which make the screen text incrementally bigger or smaller.

When you can't make the text any bigger or smaller, Movie Maker will disable the button. Different title animation styles have different limits.

10. You can also choose to change the alignment of the text on the screen. The options are left-aligned, centered, and right-aligned.

Being able to do this is useful when you are overlaying text onto a video clip, allowing you to position it over different parts of the clip. If your text is green and to the left of your picture is a hedge, for example, aligning the text to the right will allow your audience to see it more clearly.

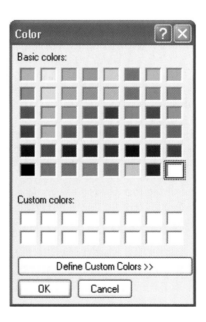

If your text fills the entire width of the screen (either by being big or too long), you may not be able to see the difference. The text here is set to centered, but you would be hard-pressed to tell the difference if it was either left- or right-aligned.

Text very close to the edges of the screen may not be shown on some televisions. Movie Maker helps you to keep within the "title safe" area, but unless it's paramount in your design, keeping text centered is safest for television output.

11. You can alter the color of both the text and, if your animation isn't overlaid onto a video clip, the background. Clicking on either of the color selection icons opens the same window.

Color:

You can choose any color you like from here. If you feel your text or background needs a color that isn't in the Basic colors: section, click on Define Custom Colors. The window will grow to show a color mixer, like those you may have seen in many image manipulation programs or even when choosing your Windows desktop colors.

12. Select your color and click OK to apply the color to your text or background.

If you are going to show your movie on a television screen eventually, be aware that certain color combinations won't display too well. It's a problem known as "banding," which has to do with the way color is reproduced by televisions. Very dark text on a light background is often a problem.

Most television programs use light text on a darker background, as this is less likely to display badly on older televisions.

13. Determine the transparency of the text to its background by adjusting the slider.

Zero percent is completely opaque (you can't see any of the background thorough the text).

Movie Maker allows you to select transparency anywhere up to 90 percent, where you will only just see the words over the background.

The Transparency control is most useful when you are creating a title to be overlaid on a video clip, but you can use it to alter how much the text stands out against any background color you select.

You can alter any or all of the title's settings as many times as you like as you experiment and preview. You can swap between the text entry, text style, and animation selection menus at any time, trying out different combinations. The current setting of your title will be shown in the preview monitor, allowing you to see just how your title will turn out.

14. When you're happy with your title, click Done, and it will appear in the timeline of your movie project. If you've decided against adding a title now (or you'd like to start over again), click Cancel.

Altering the title from your project

Once you've added a title to your movie as a clip, you can control it just as you would any other clip. You can move it around, placing it before or after other clips in both storyboard and timeline views. You can copy and paste the clip as normal.

In timeline view, you can drag it over neighboring clips to create transitions. Clip control in both views is covered in **Chapter 3**.

If you right-click on a title clip and select Edit Title... or select Edit > Edit Title... from the menu, you will be taken back to the wizard and can alter your titles as you wish.

Transparency: 0%

Transparency: 0%

Transparency: 33%

Transparency: 61%

Transparency: 90%

Trimming a title in the timeline

If you click and drag a clip to trim its length (as explained in **Chapter 3**), it will get shorter or longer as you drag.

Unlike video and audio clips that stay the same speed when you trim them (showing less or more of the clip in the movie project), trimming a title clip changes the speed of its animation.

Depending on the animation style chosen, the title may take longer to appear or scroll more slowly across the screen. Or it may simply stay on the screen longer as a still image would.

Moving a title between tracks

Title clips can be placed either on the Video track or on the Title Overlay track. If they are on the Video track, they can be manipulated as any other clip and appear with the selected background color behind them.

On Video Track   On Title Overlay Track

If they are on the Title Overlay track, they appear superimposed over the clips in the Video track, with the video showing through as the background.

You can move a title between tracks simply by dragging and dropping it. Much as if you'd moved a video clip, any clips in the Video track will shift left or right to fill any gaps created.

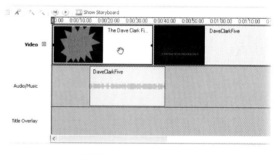

The Title Overlay track, like the Audio track, allows you to place a clip anywhere on it, meaning that you can move the title clip to any position in the movie project that you like. This allows you to have the title extend across more than one clip in the Video track.

You can overlay titles over any clip you like, including other titles—allowing you to create all manner of exciting text effects.

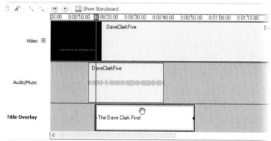

Being creative with title animations

There are already a huge variety of styles enabling you to add all sorts of titles to your movies, and more are available to download from the Internet. Check out the Microsoft web site (www.microsoft.com/windowsxp/moviemaker) for news. But you can already extend your range by adding effects to title clips or combining different animations.

Adding effects to titles

Because you can treat them like any other clip, a title in the video track can have video effects added to it.

You can watch this Pop Music Effect sample online at www.friendsofed.com.

1. Create your title clip and add it to your movie in the Video track. In this example, the title is pink Westminster text on a black background, and the animation is Stretch.

2. Open the Video Effects collection and drag an effect from the collection contents pane onto the title clip in the storyboard/timeline.

3. As with any clip, you can add multiple effects to your title clip. For the complete lowdown on video effects, see **Chapter 7**.

By adding Pixelate and Hue, Cycles Entire Color Spectrum effects, we've created something quite futuristic. The writing changes color, turns pixelated, and stretches as it fades off the screen.

Combining title animations

If you create two different title animations and place them in the timeline or storyboard one after another, you can create even more effects.

1. Create one title clip and add it to your movie in the Video track. In this example, the title is pink text in the Impact font on a black background with Spin, In as its animation.

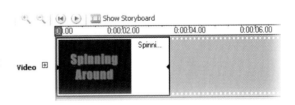

2. Copy the title, selecting it in the storyboard/ timeline and pressing CTRL+C, and then paste a copy next to it in the movie project (CTRL+V).

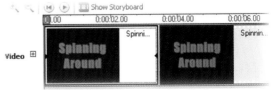

3. Right-click on the second clip and select Edit Title…. Change the title animation to another that starts with the text in the same position that the first finishes with. We've used Fade, Slow Zoom in this instance, but you can try any you like.

4. Preview the clips in the timeline. If it doesn't look quite right as the first clips fades out, you can drag the second clip to the left so it fades in over the top at the same time. Extend the second clip if you need a longer fade.

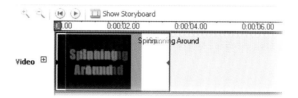

You can even add effects or alter the second clip further to create even more interesting effects.

Combining title animations on two tracks

By having two title clips running at the same time, one on the Video track and one on the Title Overlay track, you can create great dual text effects.

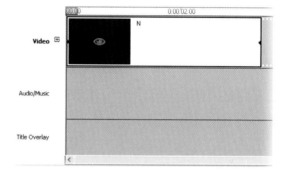

1. Create one title clip and add it to your movie in the Video track. In this example, the eye is a pink N from the Webdings font on a black background, with Zoom, Up and In as its animation.

2. Copy the title, selecting it in the storyboard/ timeline and pressing CTRL+C, then select the Title Overlay track and paste a copy (CTRL+V). Both title clips will play at exactly the same time.

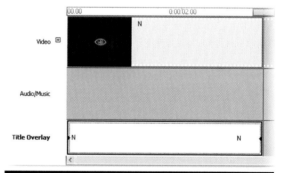

3. Edit the title in the Title Overlay track and change the animation to one you think will complement the first. Mirror works well, with the eye appearing to fly in from three positions.

You can, with a bit of ingenuity, create titles and credits to match almost any seen on TV. Some are even more simple than you think—the classic *Star Wars* opening can be created with yellow text in Arial font and Scroll, Perspective as the animation.

It's simple to create great titles with Movie Maker!

Saving and sharing movies

In this chapter

You've made your movie, be it a three-hours-long swords-and-sandals epic, or the minute-long message that you've made to e-mail to Auntie Joan. You've edited it to perfection. Now you've got to get it out there into the world.

Movie Maker 2 offers you many ways to generate and distribute your finished movie, as a file to be played on your computer, burned onto a CD, distributed across the web, or sent back to your DV camera so you have a copy on video tape. With a little ingenuity, extra software (most available to download), and the appropriate hardware, you can even make VCD and DVD discs that will play in your DVD player. In this chapter, we'll go through the process of generating to all these formats. This chapter will cover the following:

★ Video file formats and compression
★ The best options and settings for sharing your movie in different ways
★ How to use the Save Movie wizard to save your finished movie
★ Saving your movie on your computer and sending it via e-mail to the web
★ Recording your movie back to your camera on DV tape
★ Making CDs, VCDs, SVCDs, and DVDs of your movie
★ Troubleshooting to help resolve hardware and software problems

The most enjoyable thing about producing movies of any kind is being able to share them with your friends and family, so picking the right way of getting the movie to them is all-important. You may have known right from the start that you were going to e-mail your movie or burn a DVD, but all movie projects can be saved in any of the formats available. There are issues, such as file size and quality, but we'll deal with that as appropriate for each type of output. If you have any problems saving your finished movie, check the appropriate troubleshooting section at the end of the chapter.

The Save Movie wizard

To start the process of saving your finished movie, you can either select the type of output from the list in the Tasks pane or you kick off with the Save Movie wizard.

With your finished movie project open in Movie Maker, choose File > Save Movie File from the menu and the Save Movie wizard will open and ask you where you would like to save your movie.

The options here are exactly the same as those that appear in the tasks pane under the Finish Movie heading, and selecting one from here and clicking on Next will open exactly the same window.

Saving a movie to your computer

There are many reasons to save your movie as a file on your computer, including wanting to re-import the movie into Movie Maker in order to add more audio or title tracks (as discussed in **Chapters 8** and **9**), or you may want to create a VCD or DVD, which require you to use another software program. You may even just want to save your movie to play on your computer another day. Whatever the reason, you start all these processes off in the same way.

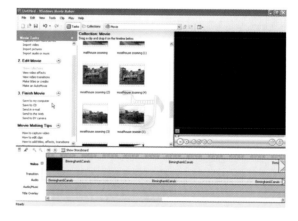

1. Select Save movie to my computer from the tasks pane or My computer from the Save Movie Wizard.

Either way, you'll be presented with the Save Movie wizard, asking you where to save your movie and what name to give it.

2. Enter a name for your movie.

The file name of the movie does not have to be the same as its title. The title, which will be displayed by some computer media players, is set in the movie project's properties box—which you can open by choosing File > Properties. For the complete lowdown on project property setting, see **Chapter 3**.

3. Choose where on your computer to save your file. You can select from a drop-down menu of common locations, or you can click Browse... to select a different folder on your machine.

You can save a movie file wherever on your computer that you like—as long as there's space.

4. Having selected a file name and a location, click on Next.

The Movie Setting window opens, which is where you can control the file size of your finished movie and the amount of **compression** that will be applied to it.

The bottom half of the window has two sections. The Movie file size section estimates the amount of space left on your chosen drive and the space that your movie will need if it's saved with the chosen settings.

The details of the settings that will be used if you click on Next are shown in the Setting details section. You can alter these (and, in effect, the estimated file size), but first you have to select Show more choices....

There are three choices here to change how you control the file settings:

★ Best quality for playback on my produces a WMV (**Windows Media Video**) file that has the highest quality possible for playing on your computer from your hard drive. You should choose this option if you're going to be watching the movie from the hard drive of your or a similar computer.

★ Best fit to file size—allows you to select a maximum file size by using the up and down arrows. You can view the file size in MB or KB, selecting either from the drop-down box. Movie Maker will change the quality settings to provide the best-quality WMV file available for that file size.

★ Other settings—allows you to select many output types from a drop-down box. These are listed by type of file needed for different kinds of playback and then by the number of bits per second of playback. You have to choose the most appropriate for your eventual playback.

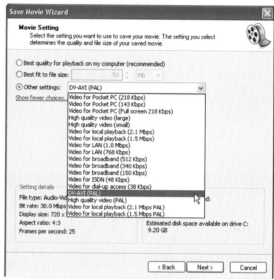

Which of these settings you choose will depend on any number of factors, but they all affect the same things about the file that will be generated: file type, bit rate, display size, aspect ratio, and number of frames per second—the things that are displayed in the Setting details section. To decide which setting to pick, let's look at each detail in turn.

File type

Movie Maker can generate two types of files: WMV, which can by played on computers that have Windows Media Player installed, and AVI (**Audio-Visual Interleaved**), which is a uncompressed video file format that produces large but best-quality files.

Very few software programs, apart from Windows Media Player, can open and use WMV files, and if you intend to open your files in another application, you need to save them as AVI.

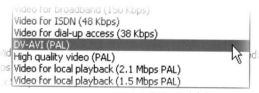

All the settings will produce WMVs of different size and quality, except DV-AVI. DV-AVI will have either (NTSC) or (PAL) after it, depending on your system settings.

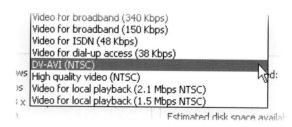

If you want to make a VCD or DVD with your movie, you will have to open it with another software package—so save it as an AVI.

Bit rate

The **bit rate** of a video file refers to the number of bits (pieces of digital information, a 1 or a 0) that need to be processed by the program that is playing back the file. Even compressed video contains thousands of bits in each frame, so this figure is normally expressed in kbps (number of kilobits per second, 1kb = 1024b) or Mbps (Megabits per second 1Mb = 1000kb).

The number of bits that can be processed by the computer on playback will depend on the speed of its CPU, the speed of its hard drive, and the speed of its Internet connection, if it needs to play the video across the web. If you want the video to be viewable by people across the Internet, select the setting that reflects the bit rate of *their* connection (select one of the Video for ISDN, broadband, or dial-up access settings)—the playback quality will be reduced accordingly.

Display size

The Display size is the size, in pixels, at which the movie will be created to be shown. The smaller the video frames are, the smaller the file size will be, but less detail will be stored. The settings that offer more compressed video files will reduce the display size.

Aspect ratio

The aspect ratio of your movie is either 4:3 (normal TV) or 16:9 (widescreen). This is set in the Options window (Tools > Options) and should be the same as the aspect ratio of the source files that were originally captured or imported.

If you change the Aspect ratio of video between capturing it and saving it as part of a finished movie, then it will be distorted.

Frames per second

The number of frames of video that are displayed every second determines how jerky or smooth the movie will appear.

NTSC video displays 30 frames per second (although the television or monitor may refresh the display more often). **PAL** video displays 25 frames per second (fps) and film is 24fps. These frame rates are high enough to be unnoticeable to the human eye.

The slower the frame, the more likely the movie is to appear jerky—but remember that the playback program has to have enough information to redraw an entire frame every time. This is why files compressed for slower computers or for showing over an Internet connection have lower frame rates—to lessen the amount of information that needs to be transferred each second.

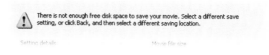

> *If there isn't enough room on your selected drive for your video to be saved with these settings, Movie Maker will tell you and won't allow you to continue.*

5. Having considered which setting will suit your playback needs best, click on Next.

Movie Maker will show you a progress bar and will estimate how much longer there is to go before it has completely saved your movie.

6. When the process is complete, you'll be asked if you'd like to play the movie when you close the wizard. If you'd like to, select this box.

7. Click on Finish. If you'd selected to watch the movie, Windows Media Player will open and play the newly saved movie. If not, you'll be returned to Movie Maker.

Your movie file is now stored on your hard disk to be copied, moved, and opened like any other file in Windows.

8. If, on watching your movie, you're not happy with the quality or file size, then you can try the save again with a different choice in the Movie Settings part of the wizard.

The issue of file size versus quality is not something that any computer program (or book!) can prescribe to you for any given situation or video. Movie Maker does a good job of making it easy to get the best quality for different circumstances by allowing you to select the destination or file size (as opposed to leaving you guessing with different **codecs**). But it can't always get it exactly right for you, so there is no shame in experimenting.

If Movie Maker's compression (or the WMV format) isn't up to scratch for your needs, you have to save your movie in AVI format (uncompressed) and invest in a program that has more control over compression and formats, such as QuickTime Pro (www.apple.com).

Saving your movie to a CD

Most computers these days are equipped with a CD-R drive that is capable of **burning** (recording) information onto blank CDs. Movie Maker makes it easy to burn your movie onto a CD, one that is specially compressed to play back well on any computer on which Windows Media Player is installed.

It uses a format called **HighMAT** encoding, which gives very good quality video and audio. Microsoft hopes that in the future, many manufacturers will enable their DVD players to play HighMAT format CDs, but at present, you will only be able to play these on Windows computers and certain new Panasonic machines. If you are very interested in this, you could check out www.highmat.com.

1. With your finished movie project open, insert a recordable CD into your CD-R or CD-RW drive. Start the process either by using the Save Movie wizard, or by selecting Save to CD from the tasks pane.

If you attempt to start the creation process without a CD in the drive, you'll see a warning something like this:

2. You will be asked to type in a name for your saved movie, or you can accept the default.

3. You can also enter a name for the CD itself. CD names have to be shorter than movie names, and you are restricted to 16 characters.

Save Movie Wizard

Insert a recordable or rewriteable CD to continue.

⚠ There is no disc in the recordable CD drive.

Insert a recordable CD into drive E:\.

Save Movie Wizard

Saved Movie File
Enter information for your saved movie file.

1. Enter a file name for your saved movie.

Birmigham & Its Canals

2. Enter a name for the CD.

Birmigham & Its

4. After naming your movie and CD, click OK.

You will be shown the Movie Setting options, which are similar but slightly different to those that you see when saving a movie to your computer.

5. If you are intending to save only one movie to this CD, select the Best fit for recordable CD option. This will allow Movie Maker to use as little compression as possible, while still keeping the movie small enough to fit on a CD.

Most CDs can hold 650MB of data, if your movies are smaller than that you can fit more than one on each disc.

6. If you would like to fit more than one movie on a CD or need to keep the file size low for another reason, you can select Best fit to file size and control the size of your movie directly.

7. The Other settings, which you can select from the drop-down box, allow you to control the bit rate of the saved movie. You would use one of these options if you knew that the movie would eventually be watched on a slow computer or across a network, choosing the highest setting that could be played on that system.

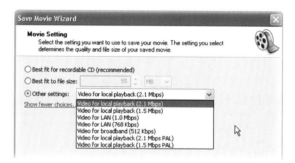

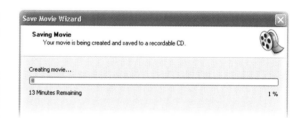

8. When you've selected the appropriate Movie Setting, click OK and sit back and watch Movie Maker create your movie and burn it onto CD.

Movie Maker keeps you informed of the different parts of the process—creating the movie, preparing the movie for saving to the CD (compressing it and encoding into HighMAT format), and finally burning it onto the CD. The whole process could take a while, depending on the speed of your CD-RW drive.

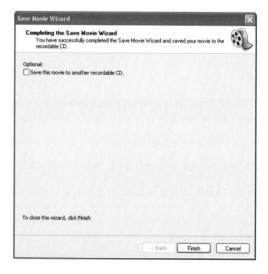

9. When your CD has been finalized, you are asked if you would like to save the same movie to another CD. This is useful if you are intending to make multiple copies, because it will save you from having to wait for Movie Maker to compress and encode the same movie all over again.

10. Eject your CD. It will now play automatically when you put it into a computer on which Windows Media Player is installed.

Sending a video by e-mail

E-mail is an ideal way of sharing movies with family and friends across the world. Movie Maker will compress your movie so it small enough to be easily e-mailed and even start your default mail program for you to send it along with your message.

File size

The biggest issue with sending a movie by e-mail is file size. Most **ISP**s, or mail service providers, restrict the size of any **attachments**; MSN's free Hotmail service only allows users to receive attachments of up to 1MB. Even the most powerful broadband services will restrict the attachment size that can be sent or received, so 10MB would be an absolute upper limit.

You can set the maximum file size for e-mailed movies from the Options dialog box (Tools > Options). Click on the Advanced tab, and the E-mail setting is at the bottom of the box.

If you want to make sure that everyone will be able to receive the movie, leave this set at 1MB. If you know that your audience has mail accounts with larger limits, you can push this figure up.

> *Even if your audience can receive large attachments, the attachments can cause problems with e-mail servers—a good upper size limit to use is 2MB.*

With a very small file size limit, quality will inevitably suffer. Movie Maker will do its best to get the best quality available (making the size of the video smaller on screen, reducing the frame rate) but there's a limit to what a computer can do.

Reducing file size when editing

Sometimes, even when applying the maximum amount of compression, Movie Maker will not be able to make your movie fit under the size limit. Here, a movie that is three minutes, 38 seconds long will not compress to less than 1MB. Keeping your movie short is the key factor here.

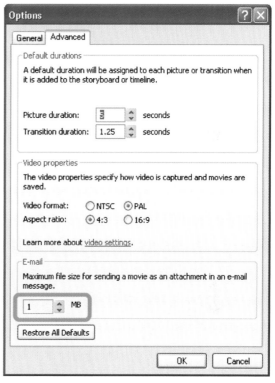

Trimming the movie at both ends, losing only some time with credits on screen (also cutting some of the soundtrack) to three minutes, 18 seconds lets Movie Maker slip in at just under 1MB.

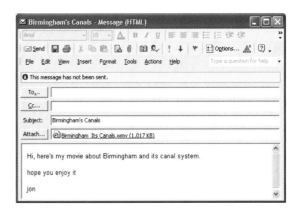

> *File size is also increased by movement on screen, so sharp pans or zooms will make it harder for Movie Maker to compress your movie well.*

Saving your movie to send via e-mail

When you've edited your movie, you're ready to send it as an e-mail. You need to have the project file open in Movie Maker.

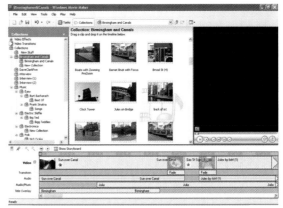

1. Check your default maximum e-mail size (Tools > Options), alter it if you have to, and click OK.

2. Start the process by either selecting Send in e-mail from the Finish Movie section of the tasks pane or starting the Save Movie wizard (File > Save Movie...) and selecting E-mail.

Movie Maker will now estimate how much it will need to compress the movie in order to make your maximum file size for e-mail. If it cannot compress it enough, you will see this box.

3. You can adjust the maximum e-mail size in this box by changing the value in the Do not warn me again... box. If you change this value, it will become your default maximum e-mail file size.

4. Change the size limit here, or go back and edit your movie slightly if you don't want to alter the file size limit. When you've made changes to the movie project, start again from step 2.

Movie Maker then saves and compresses your movie file, showing you a progress bar as it does so.

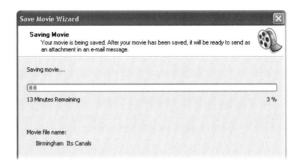

When it has finished the movie creation process, it offers you options to save a copy of the movie onto your hard drive and to play a copy of it when the wizard finishes.

5. If you would like to send this movie from an e-mail address that isn't your default account (e.g. your Hotmail account), you'll need to save your movie to your hard drive—so click on the Save a copy of my movie on my computer link. You'll be presented with the familiar file browser.

It's also useful to save a copy of the movie somewhere on your computer in case you want to watch it yourself later or to have in case the email doesn't reach one of your friends.

6. If you'd like a preview of the movie before you send it, click on Play the movie. This is a good idea because you've not seen this compressed version yet.

7. Click on Next, and Movie Maker will open an e-mail with your movie already attached. You can fill in the To field with your friends' e-mail addresses and edit the rest of your message as you see fit. It's best to tell your friends what type of file you've sent them and what it's about.

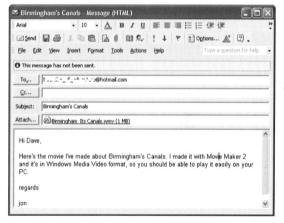

8. If they already have Windows Media Player installed on their computer, they should be able to play the movie without any problems. If you think that they may not, you can include a link to the Microsoft web site where they will be able to download the latest version.

9. Click on Send and your movie should wing its way across the Internet to your audience.

If you are not connected to the Internet, your movie will be sent the next time that you connect and send e-mail. If you have any problems with this process, check the troubleshooting section later in this chapter.

The URL is www.microsoft.com/windows/ windowsmedia/9series/player.aspx.

Sending to the web

If you have a lot of people that you'd to like to watch your movie, then the best option may be to send it to be hosted on the web. This will allow, in theory, anyone in the world to see it (as long as you let them know exactly where it is!).

Instead of directly e-mailing all your friends copies of your movie to watch, you could send one copy to a **web host** (place that stores Internet content) and e-mail your friends a message that includes a link to the **URL** (web address). This also means that you don't have to squeeze your movie to fit e-mail file size limits, so it can be better quality.

If you do this, send us an e-mail with a link, too (or if you really want to show off, post a link on our online forums at www.friendsofed.com)—we'd love to see what you've made.

Anyone can use the wizard to get their movies optimized and compressed especially for watching across the Internet—and then upload them to their own web space.

A word of warning now. Only some parts of the world have web-hosting providers that are set up with Movie Maker at the time of this writing. You will have to create an account (and pay a fee) to use those that are available. If you're in the US, you can use this wizard to send movies directly to the web with providers such as Neptune Mediashare (which charges a $39 joining fee).

1. With your movie project open in Movie Maker, select Send to the Web from the tasks pane or open the Save Movie wizard.

2. Enter a file name for your movie, and click Next. This name will be the file name of the finished movie, so it's best to give it one that identifies it to everyone.

3. The Movie Setting window offers options here that control the format and compression of the movie. They are listed by type and speed of Internet connection.

4. If you click on Show more choices, you can also control the file size directly, as well as having many more Internet connection speeds to choose from.

The choice here is about the connection speed of the eventual viewers—if they are all your friends and you know what type of Internet access they have, then it's easy—you can just select the closest one.

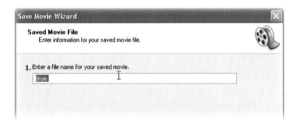

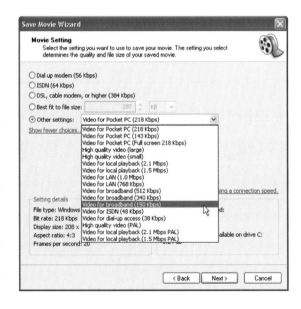

If you're not sure of the Internet set-up of your target audience, it's more tricky. You have to decide whether it is more important that more people can watch your movie easily—or whether the quality is more important.

Quite simply, the choices with the higher bit rate (as explained in the "Saving a movie to your computer" section of this chapter) will produce better quality movie files. The downside is that the size of the files will be larger, and as the bit rate rises, fewer people will be able to watch your film without pauses and jerks as their player buffers the data.

5. Choose your Movie Setting. Click Next, and watch and wait as Movie Maker creates your movie.

6. Movie Maker will now connect to the web and check if there are web-hosting providers available to you. If you are not connected to the Internet, you should connect now.

7. Assuming there is a hosting provider available in your area, you'll see this page. Click sign up now to see a list of providers available. You will have to sign up for an account with a provider, if you want to distribute your movie in this way.

8. Once you have an account with a video hosting provider, enter in your user name and password.

9. Click Next, and Movie Maker will transfer your video to the web. This may take some time, depending on the speed of your connection.

10. You can then select the Watch my movie on the Web... box, and you will get a preview of how your audience will see your movie.

11. If there are no hosts available that allow direct uploading for people in your area, you will see this message:

12. Select the option to Save a copy of my movie on my computer, and a file browser will open. Save the movie file somewhere on your hard drive.

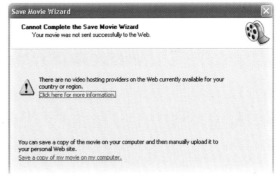

You will now have a WMV file that is ready for uploading to your own personal webspace. There are so many different types of host and methods of transfer that it is impossible to explain them all here. Your web service provider or ISP will have instructions on their web site.

Sending to DV tape

By transferring your finished movie to digital videotape, you gain a huge degree of flexibility—you can play that tape in any other camera that accepts them. You can connect your camera to almost any television and watch your movie, complete with titles and effects, on the big screen. You can also connect your camera to a video recorder and make copies on VHS (or even Betamax) for your friends and family.

Temporary file size

Before Movie Maker records to your tape, a temporary file will be saved to your hard drive. This file will be very large, so you should set its location (on the General tab in the Options window—Tools > Options) to the hard drive with the most space available, if you have more than one. Some disk configurations also have a limited file size.

If the temporary file for your movie would be too large for your disk, you will have to split your movie into two or more parts and record them one after another onto your DV tape.

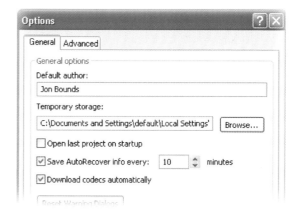

Saving your movie to DV tape

Having set your temporary file size and edited your movie, you're ready to go.

1. Connect your camera to the FireWire port on your computer. If you've been capturing footage earlier, it may already be connected. To save problems later, it's best to have your camera plugged in to an electrical socket while recording.

2. To record a tape in your DV camera, you will need to check that your camera is in either **VCR**, **VTR**, or **playback mode**. What it is called will depend on your particular camera. Check your manual for details, but it will probably look something like this diagram:

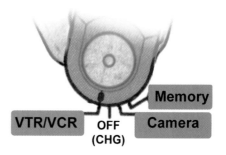

3. With your movie project open, start the recording process by clicking on Send to DV Camera in the tasks pane. Or start the Save Movie wizard.

4. Movie Maker will prompt you to to cue your tape, which means to make sure that it's at the right point to begin recording. Use the controls on the camera to fast-forward or rewind the tape to the point where you want to begin recording your movie.

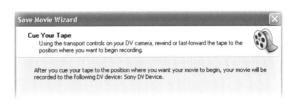

Look at the length of your movie and make sure that you have enough tape available to record all of it.

5. Click on Next when you have the tape at the right point. You will see this warning:

6. Just as with a video recorder or an audio cassette, it's possible to record over other footage on DV tape. Make sure that there's nothing important on the tape you're using. Click Yes when you're ready.

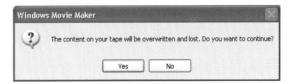

7. Your movie will begin saving onto your computer and then will be recorded onto the DV tape in your camcorder. As ever, Movie Maker shows you a progress bar, but this time there's something more interesting to do: you can watch the screen on your DV camera while the movie is being recorded to the tape.

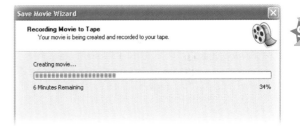

8. After the movie has finished being recorded onto the tape, the temporary file that was created in the process will be deleted from your hard drive. You can disconnect your camera and click Finish to close the dialog box.

Now that you've got your movie on a DV tape, you can connect the camera to your TV and watch it in comfort.

Creating a VCD or DVD

Though you cannot directly create a DVD with Movie Maker, it's not that difficult to use another piece of software (such as the one that came with your DVD-R drive) to create a DVD with the movie files that Movie Maker produces.

If you own Sonic MyDVD 4 (www.mydvd.com), then it's even easier, because the program has been specially written to accept WMV files and comes with full documentation that explains the process. Unfortunately, there isn't a demo version of this software to download to try before you buy.

If you haven't got a DVD-R (or DVD+R, which is a slightly different format) drive, then you can't record a DVD with your computer. Anyone who has a CD-R (much more common) can still create VCDs (**Video Compact Discs**) and SVCDs (Super Video Compact Discs) which, although they can't store as much information, will play back on many DVD players with similar high-quality digital output.

The process of making all these kinds of discs is very similar, and we'll go through them all at the same time. A great deal of VCD and DVD creation advice is available at www.dvdrhelp.com.

Preparing the movie for VCD or DVD

Very few non-Microsoft software packages support WMV files, and Movie Maker cannot export as MPEG compressed files—the type that VCDs and DVDs need. We need to save our movie files and then convert them into the right format.

1. Save your movie to your computer as an AVI file (which will be DV-AVI [NTSC] or DV-AVI (PAL), depending on your TV standards. Don't worry if the file size that Movie Maker creates is larger that 650MB (for a CD) or 4GB (for a DVD) because it will be compressed before it is burned onto the disc.

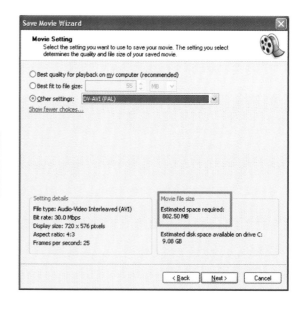

> *All these sorts of discs use MPEG compression. VCDs use MPEG 1 compression and SVCDs and DVDs use MPEG 2.*

To compress and covert your movie to an MPEG file, we recommend the program TMPGEnc (www.tmpgenc.net/e_main.html). Download it and you are able to convert AVI files to MPEG 1 for free. MPEG 2 compression is limited to a 30–day trial period.

2. Open TMPGEnc and you'll be presented with the Project wizard—just what you need to convert your file.

3. Select your disc type from the list on the left and TMPGEnc will show you the details of its required file format, including VCD, SVCD, and DVD in both NTSC and PAL formats. Click Next when you've selected the correct one.

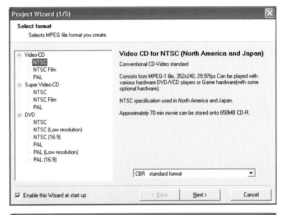

4. Click the Browse button to select your video file. Pick your movie file from the file browser that opens, and remember that you want the AVI file we've just created.

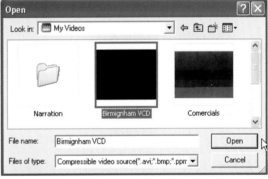

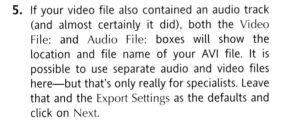

5. If your video file also contained an audio track (and almost certainly it did), both the Video File: and Audio File: boxes will show the location and file name of your AVI file. It is possible to use separate audio and video files here—but that's only really for specialists. Leave that and the Export Settings as the defaults and click on Next.

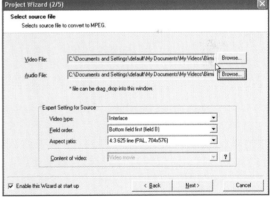

6. It is also wise to leave the default settings on the next two Project wizard steps, Filter settings and Bitrate settings, by clicking Next on each. The default settings are fine for most purposes and you can ruin the whole process by making unnecessary alterations.

7. Choose a file name and location for your MPEG file using the file browser. Click Next.

8. You can then watch your movie as the encoding process takes place. When it's finished, close TMPGEnc, and you're ready to burn.

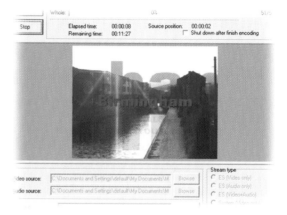

Creating a VCD or SVCD

Most CD creation software is capable of creating a VCD or SVCD. If you don't already have one that does, you can download a trial version of Nero, without doubt the most popular CD burning software, which functions for 30 days (from www.nero.com).

Here we'll run through the process of making a VCD or SVCD with Nero. The choices and decisions will be similar if you decide to use another burning program.

1. Open Nero, and if you're not shown this wizard, open it with File > New. Select the Compile a new CD option and click Next.

2. Nero makes many different types of CD. We're making a Video CD, so select that and click Next.

3. Nero will set up the VCD for you and open a window for you to customize it and add video files. When you are ready to start this process, click Finish.

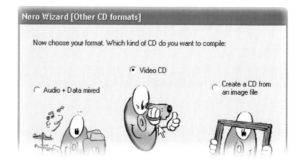

4. Locate the MPEG file of your movie in the file browser window. Select it and drag it into the main window of the VCD.

Nero won't let you add files to the VCD that aren't of the right type. It will accept AVI files, but Nero's conversion and compression software is not as powerful as that of TMPGEnc, so it's still best to convert your files first.

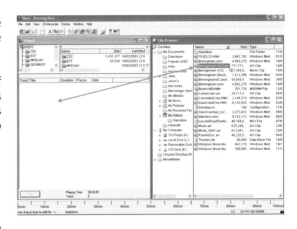

5. You can add as many movie files as will fit on your VCD. When you've added enough or it's full, click on the button to open the Write-CD dialog box.

You are given the choice of making a test run, testing and then burning your CD, or going straight to burning. (The test simulates the burn to see if your CD-R drive will be able to keep up rather than ruin a blank disc by failing midway.)

6. If you're feeling confident, click Burn and go for it.

Nero will encode your video and burn your VCD, ejecting the disc when finished. Your VCD will then be playable in many, but not all, DVD players. Sadly, some (especially earlier) players cannot play these discs—see the section on troubleshooting later in this chapter.

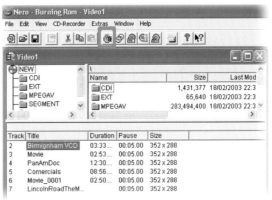

Making a DVD

Not only do you need software to burn the DVD, you also need some that will create the menus that you see on screen, and the software that came supplied with your DVD-R drive may not be up to the task. MyDVD is one option; ULead's DVD MovieFactory 2 is another and has the virtue of having a fully functioning demo version available for download from www.ulead.com/dmf. The process of creation should be similar in all packages.

1. So that anyone who wants to follow this exercise can, we're going to use MovieFactory 2. Download a trial version and install it.

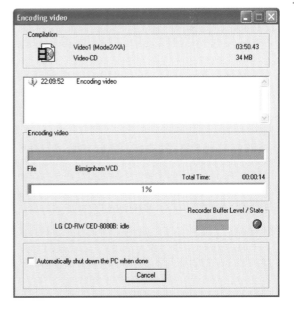

2. Open MovieFactory and you'll see that it is a wizard based piece of software, which should make it simple for you to use.

3. Click Start Project from the left buttons and New project and DVD from the main panel. Click Next.

4. This window is where all the DVD creation is done. You can add video files by clicking on the Add Video icon and even preview them in the file browser to make sure you've selected the right one.

DVD MovieFactory allows you to capture video direct from your DV camera, edit it, and export it within the same program. Not all DVD creation packages can do this, and few can perform anywhere near as well as Movie Maker as an editing package—so here we're only going to import files to create our DVD.

5. Import your MPEG 2 movie file (again, MovieFactory will allow you to import some other types, but it's wise to use a dedicated program like TMPGEnc to do the encoding) and it will sit at the bottom of the window, looking much like it was in Movie Maker's storyboard. You can add as many files as will fit on a DVD.

In many DVD creation packages, you can add **Chapter Markers** to your video files. These are points in the movie that viewers can jump to by using the track skip >>| and |<< buttons on the DVD player and also by navigating the menus.

6. If you would like to include this feature in your DVD, select your video in the storyboard and click on Add/Edit Chapter. You can then preview your movie (in much the same way as in Movie Maker's preview monitor) and click on Add (to add chapter markers at the current point). Click OK to return to the main screen.

7. If you would like to have the movie run automatically when a disc is inserted, select the First clip as first play video box. Note that this will not allow you to have a menu.

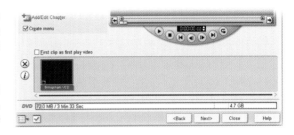

8. When you're happy with all your clips and chapters and you're ready to add your menu, click on Next (making sure that the Create menu box is selected).

9. In the menu creation window, you can customize almost anything you want about the menus—changing the background image and adding background music, entering a title for the disc and choosing its font size and color. You can also change which part of the movie file is shown as its representational thumbnail—useful if your movie fades in from black.

In MovieFactory you just click on something to alter its look and feel—it's very easy.

10. Each separate movie file can also have a submenu (chapter menu) from which the user can select different parts to watch—and those menus are equally as changeable. If you'd rather not have chapter menus, you can clear the Add Chapter Menus box.

11. When you're completely happy with your menu system, click on Next. You are then taken to a preview window. The controls at the bottom act just like the controls on a DVD player, and you can use them to test the menu system and the movies. If you find a problem, click Back to go back and refine your menus. If you're satisfied, click Next.

This is the window where you finally burn your DVD:

12. Give it a Volume name. You won't be allowed to exceed the 32-character limit.

13. In the Output settings section, select the Record to Disc box, and select DVD-Video as the Recording format.

14. Select your DVD-R/DVD+R drive as the Drive in the Disc burner section.

15. And you're ready to burn. Place your blank DVD in the drive and click on the Output icon.

Obviously this isn't a totally in-depth tutorial on using DVD MovieFactory—that could take a whole book in itself—but it should be enough to get you going and burning your first DVD.

Troubleshooting Movie Maker 2

Creating and sending movies is one of the most resource-heavy tasks that you can ask your computer to do. So if Movie Maker crashes (either when saving movies or at other times), first try closing other programs and running Movie Maker on its own. If problems persist, the two most common reasons for crashes and lockups are the computer's hardware acceleration setting and Movie Maker clashing with AX files installed by other software.

You can test either or both fairly easily and quickly without rebooting.

Hardware acceleration

1. Right-click anywhere on the Desktop background and choose Properties.

2. In the Display properties box, select the Settings tab.

3. Click on the Advanced button.

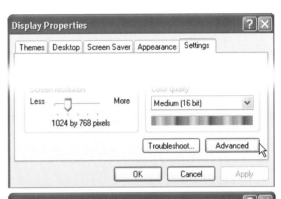

4. In the dialog box that opens, click on the Troubleshoot tab.

The Hardware acceleration: slider goes in six notches from None to Full. The positions correspond to the following:

★ None—Disable all accelerations.
★ Disable all but basic accelerations.
★ Disable all DirectDraw and Direct3D acceleration, as well as all cursor and advanced drawing accelerations.
★ Disable all cursor and advanced drawing accelerations. Use this setting to correct drawing problems.
★ Disable cursor and bitmap accelerations.
★ Full—All accelerations are enabled.

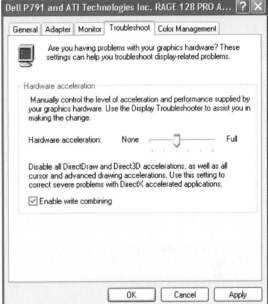

5. Change your Hardware acceleration to the third position, because DirectDraw problems can cause Movie Maker to crash.

Clashing with AX files

A review of the thousands of posts to the microsoft.public.windowsxp.moviemaker newsgroup shows that Movie Maker can clash with one or more of seven AX files. AX files (those with an `.ax` extension) are DirectShow Filters and MPEG-4 DVD Filters (which are multimedia codecs).

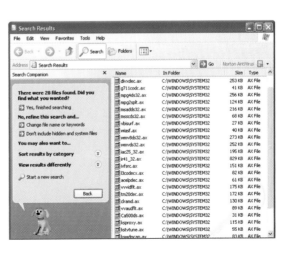

1. Find all the AX files on your computer. Choose Search from the Start menu to search for files with an `.ax` extension, using the All files and folders option. Remember to include system and hidden files.

2. Check if you have any of these seven:

- ★ `claud.ax`—an MPEG codec redistributed by PowerDVD—checkCyberlink(www.gocyberlink.com/english/download) for a patch that resolves this `PDVDxp4_Patch_2417.exe`.
- ★ `clvsd.ax`—an MPEG codec redistributed by PowerDVD.
- ★ `cmaudio.ax`—from C-Media Inc. (sound card or audio chip).
- ★ `divxaf.ax`—Digital Anti-Freeze—part of the Nimo codec package—causes crashes when trying to preview or play transitions and effects.
- ★ `iviaudio.ax`—ships with WinDVD and may be installed more than once in a couple of folders. This affects MP3 files that are larger than 160kbps, causing sped-up audio, chipmunk sounds, and clipping sounds.
- ★ `subtitds.ax`—installed by SLD codec pack in the `System32` folder.
- ★ `wtwmplug.ax`—associated with Wild Tangent games.

3. Rename them, changing the file extension to something like `.ax_`, and then see if Movie Maker improves its performance.

It's best first to rename all and any of the seven you have, in case Movie Maker clashes with more than one.

4. If Movie Maker works okay after you rename them, you might rename them back, one at a time, until you determine which one(s) are clashing.

If renaming these files doesn't resolve your issue, you might try renaming additional AX files. Look for new ones each time you install a new program.

If you find that renaming another AX file resolves your problem, please let us know by sending us an e-mail (support@friendsofed.com) so that we can help others in the same situation.

Do not delete these files! They have been installed by another piece of software onto your system—you may need to rename them back to use that program.

Troubleshooting saving movies

Creating and saving movies requires a great deal of space on your computer's hard drive and a large amount of processing power. Clear as much space on your hard drive as possible and defragment it (All Programs > Accessories > System Tools > Disk Defragmenter from the Start menu) if necessary.

Close all other programs because attempting to save a movie while other programs are running may cause dropped frames in the finished movie.

Problems with the Save Movie wizard

You might see this warning when you attempt to save or send a movie:

There are a number of problems that could have caused this warning. Some are obvious, some are not.

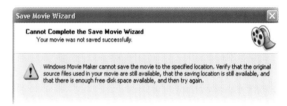

1. First, check that you haven't moved or renamed any of your source files. Remember, if you've imported files into your collections from a removable disk (CD, Zip, or floppy), that disk must be available when you attempt to save your finished movie.

2. Second, check the amount of space on the drive on which you are trying to save the movie—it is possible that there isn't enough room. Try Start > All Programs > Accessories> System Tools > Disk Cleanup to free some space.

If neither of those appear to fix the problem (or you're sure you haven't moved the source files and you've enough space to save the movie file), it may be down to the way you've installed Movie Maker.

3. Reinstall Movie Maker (don't worry, your collections will remain intact), not from Windows Update, but directly from the Microsoft web site: www.microsoft.com/ windowsxp/moviemaker/downloads /moviemaker2.asp.

> *This is especially useful if you have previously installed Movie Maker from Windows Update and the problems have started since you installed other software.*

Problems saving long movies

You may have problems saving longer movies, especially those more than five minutes long; your system might hang during the saving process.

If this happens, install the newest version of Direct Draw (version 9 is said to solve most problems). To do this, use Windows Update (All Programs > Windows Update from the Start menu).

Troubleshooting sending e-mail

If you have completed the Save Movie wizard for sending your movie by e-mail and an e-mail message doesn't appear for you to edit and send, it may be because your default e-mail program does not support automatic attachments, or you may not have one selected.

You will see a warning like this:

You have two choices: either you save a copy of your movie onto your computer and then use your e-mail program to attach the movie to an e-mail message, or you change your e-mail program and try the saving process again.

Changing your e-mail program

Your default e-mail program (along with other Internet settings) is specified in the Internet Options box. To change your default e-mail program, do the following:

1. From the Start menu, choose Control Panel. In Classic view, double-click on the Internet Options icon.

2. The Internet Properties dialog box will open. Select the Programs tab.

3. In the E-mail: drop-down box, the current default e-mail program name is displayed. To specify a new default e-mail program, choose an e-mail program from the list.

4. Click OK to save your choices.

> *Microsoft Outlook, Outlook Express, and Hotmail all support direct attachments.*

5. Go back to Movie Maker, and try sending your movie by e-mail again.

Your e-mails aren't being received

Normally, if your e-mails don't get through, you will receive an automated response from a mail server. This will detail the reasons that it couldn't deliver the message, which will usually be that the e-mail address was incorrect. (Check the spelling!)

You may also receive a response that tells you that your message couldn't be delivered because the attachment was too big. In these cases, reduce the size of your maximum e-mail file size in Movie Maker and try again. If you don't get an automated failure notice, you can't always assume your mail has gotten through—some servers do not send them. Be warned.

Troubleshooting saving to a CD

Saving your movie to a CD should be a trouble-free process, as long as you have a compatible CD-R drive and a blank CD.

Checking your CD-R drive

If your CD-R drive is correctly installed and set up in Windows XP, you shouldn't have any problems.

1. Open My Computer and right-click on the drive and choose Properties. Click on the Recording tab.

2. Make sure that the box that says Enable CD recording on this drive is selected. Click OK.

If this doesn't solve your problem, the difficulty may be with your CD-R's drivers and installation.

1. Open the Device Manager (double-click on the System button in the Control Panel and click the Hardware tab and then the Device Manager button). Right-click on the icon for your CD-R drive and choose Propeties.

2. In the drive's properties window, click on the Driver tab. Try letting Windows search for a more up-to-date driver by clicking on the Update Driver button.

If Windows doesn't find a better driver or it has and you are still having problems, return to the CD-R drive's properties window and try the Troubleshooter (on the General tab).

Problems writing to a CD

If you do not start from a completely blank CD, Movie Maker may have problems recording to it.

If the disc has been created or written to with another software program (e.g., Nero), it may be in the wrong format. Movie Maker will write only to discs that are multisession, Joliet (Mode 2) format.

Make sure that any software you use to burn CDs uses Joliet (Mode 2) and not ISO 9660 (Mode 1) format—you can normally set this in the program's options.

If you are trying to save more that one movie to a CD with Movie Maker and it won't allow you, this may be because the disc is full. Movie Maker will finalize (close for writing) any CD that has less than 50MB of space left on it. So, even though there may have been room for your last movie, you cannot save it. If you know space is going to be tight, burn your biggest movie last (as long as it is more than 50MB) to prevent this from happening.

Troubleshooting saving to DV tape

Saving to DV tape can be problematic because there are not only software and computer issues, but potential pitfalls with your camera, the tape, and the connecting leads as well.

Hardware checks

Check that your camera is turned on and that the FireWire lead connecting to the camera is securely in the correct ports at both ends.

Power your camera from an electrical outlet when possible (this may prevent your camera from switching into standby or power-saving mode)—or at least make sure the battery is fully charged.

Make sure that the tape has its write-protect tab set to the record position.

Make sure that your video camera is in VCR/VTR or playback mode. Switch the camera off completely, and then switch it into this mode.

If you're in Europe or your camera was bought from there, check the manual whether it supports DV-In as well as DV-Out. Some cameras supplied in the European Union have their DV-In capabilities disabled due to tax and import duties. It can be re-enabled if you know what you're doing with electronics—check out the information page at www.dv-in.com for detailed information.

Troubleshooting making VCDs and DVDs

If you've managed to create a VCD or DVD with your movie with whatever software you have, it's unlikely that there's something wrong with the disc.

More likely is that the DVD player on which you are attempting to watch the disc is incompatible with CD-R or DVD-R discs. Most newer players are compatible, and almost all DVD drives connected to computer systems will work.

> *A nearly complete and ever growing list of compatible players can be found at* www.dvdrhelp.com/dvdplayers.php.

If your player is listed as compatible and the disc still won't work, it's possible that it was corrupted as it was burned. This is more likely to happen if you ran other programs on your computer as the burning program was working. Try one more time, running nothing else. If your disc still fails to work, there may be a hardware fault with either your CD-R/DVD-R or your DVD player.

Sharing your movies

However you choose to share the movie that you've made with Movie Maker, you can be sure that your friends and family will be impressed.

If you've added transitions, effects, and titles to your work, you'll no doubt get at least one "Wow! How did you do that?" You should feel justifiably proud.

We've tried to add as much information as we can, in this chapter particularly, to help you solve any problems you might encounter because it would be incredibly frustrating not to be able to show your masterpiece to the people you've made it for.

To help you move on from simply editing and distributing video to really creating movies that you'll be proud of in years to come, the rest of the book is devoted to four pro-standard projects that have been completed in Movie Maker.

If you get stuck following them, then you should be able to refer back to the appropriate section in the book, using the index and table of contents as a guide. If you're still having difficulties, don't forget that you can e-mail our support team.

E-mailing a video postcard

Jen deHaan

In this chapter

Making and sending a "video postcard" by e-mail is a perfect project to start with. You can use video clips (from your camcorder, old home movies, even TV and computer screen-captures if you have permission), still images (from your digital camera, scanner, or the Internet), and selections from your personal music library.

The plan is to merge camcorder footage and digital still pictures taken at a traditional New Year's Eve get-together. We'll need Movie Maker 2 to capture the camcorder clips to the computer, edit them, and produce the final movie.

We'll then use Movie Maker to initiate the e-mail process and distribute the movie as an e-mail attachment to family and friends. This chapter will cover the following:

★ Capturing digital and analog camcorder video clips
★ Importing digital still pictures
★ Importing a music track
★ Editing the movie to a maximum two-minute running time
★ Generating our movie at a file size suitable for an e-mail
★ Initiating the e-mail by using Movie Maker

Project constraints

Each project has its own constraints, even if self-imposed, and they provide a framework for the project, helping you work in an effective and efficient manner.

Think about who your intended audience is and how the world of digital multimedia looks from their perspective. Sometimes your audience will set some of the constraints—a family member without a computer will need a VCR tape, VCD, or DVD to view your movie.

The WMV files produced by Movie Maker run only under Windows Media Player 7 or later. The e-mail message that is included in Movie Maker provides the receiver with a link to update their Windows Media Player if needed. This may help, but it won't help those who cannot use newer versions of the Windows Media Player, which includes anyone whose computer still runs Windows 95 or earlier.

The audience

Three couples were at the New Year's Eve get-together used for this video postcard, and they are the primary audience for the finished version. Two have high-speed cable connections to the Internet: one uses Windows XP; the other, Windows 98. The third has a slow modem connection and Windows 95. I wasn't sure they could view this project without upgrading, so I will have to invite them over to see it on my computer or put a copy of it on videotape.

For this video postcard, all the constraints are self-imposed:

★ The final movie will have a file size no larger than 1MB, which is a suitable size to e-mail. It shouldn't take longer than three minutes to download over a 56k modem and will of course be much quicker over a broadband or ADSL connection.

> *Remember that some e-mail services do not allow attachments that are more than 1MB, including the basic Hotmail service.*

★ The final movie will have a two-minute maximum running time. Any larger and the quality of the finished movie will drop excessively because we will have to use too much compression. Two minutes is also comparable to the amount of time it would take to read a conventional, written postcard.

Your target audience will be different. It's a great idea to think about them before starting.

Planning and preparation

I bought a new pack of camcorder video tapes, fully charged the camera batteries, set the camcorder tapes to be at the right positions to start filming, and checked that the flash cards for the digital still camera were empty.

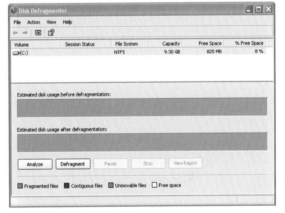

Having enough free hard drive space and "**defragging**" the hard drives before doing video work can prevent many potential problems. As part of my getting ready for any new video project, I always clean up my hard drive. The Windows Disk Defragmenter can be found on the Start menu at Start > All Programs > Accessories > System Tools > Disk Defragmenter.

Music choice

I browsed through my music collection for an appropriate background music selection. I only needed one piece and the New Year's theme helped me chose a cut version of "Auld Lang Syne."

You can speed up or slow down video playback on selected clips and easily change the speed of the video, but the speed of the music is fixed at real time. Your choice of music has considerable impact on the overall movie.

Filming the event

After arriving at the get-together, I told everyone about making the video this year. I was using two camcorders and a still digital camera.

Head-based editing (known as in-camera editing) was a habit I developed before the days of digital, nonlinear editing, when anything done in the camcorder saved time putting a finished movie together.

Breaking this habit allows me to participate and enjoy the event fully while producing a much better movie.

Lighting

Most of the rooms were dark, lit mainly by candlelight. It was a wonderful atmosphere but difficult for video. The last thing I wanted to do was to turn on a bright light to take better video. Doing so could turn a relaxed cozy setting into a video production environment.

I had both a digital and a Hi8 camcorder with me and decided to use the Hi8 for the darker scenes and the digital for lighter ones. In my experience, my Hi8 camera worked better in low-light situations than the digital camcorder.

The normal flash of a still camera doesn't detract from the atmosphere. Everyone is used to such flashes, and the images are much better to use in the movie than still pictures from a camcorder or captured frames from the video.

Movement and compression

Compression of video files is affected by various factors and, with our constraint on file size, clips with lots of action in them would result in compression problems. So I was careful to use a tripod wherever I could. Sometimes only the flickering of a candle shows you that it is a video clip and not a still picture, but that flickering is all you need to enhance the overall feeling when watching the movie.

I ended up with more than 40 minutes of video footage, which would easily be sufficient for a two-minute movie. The only thing that was close to being staged was having each person say "Happy New Year" to the camcorder. Someone else had to film me, of course!

Video shot in candlelight

Still image using flash

Capturing from digital camcorder

My computer has an internal FireWire card, and I keep a FireWire cable plugged into it, waiting for a digital camcorder to be connected.

The digital camcorder is a Sony TRV330—NTSC, which plays both digital and Hi8 and 8mm analog tapes. When capturing, I use its external power adapter to avoid any low-battery situations.

Even with the FireWire cable plugged into the camcorder and the camcorder's power switch turned on, the computer doesn't notice the camcorder. But, as soon as the switch is turned to the VCR position, a Digital Video Device window opens on the computer, with Windows Movie Maker being one of the choices. After selecting Movie Maker and pressing OK, Movie Maker opens and the Video Capture wizard starts.

Notice how the wizard knows that the camcorder is a Sony DV device.

Use the Browse... button and then Make New Folder to create a new folder for the video files that will be captured from the camcorder. This is good practice whenever capturing a new batch of footage.

After the folder is created, click OK to return to the previous window, and you'll see the new location for the video to be captured. When you're satisfied that you've selected the right directory, choose Next to open the Video Setting window.

For the video setting, the default of Best quality for playback on my computer would work fine for this project. However, I select Digital device format (DV-AVI) to capture at the highest quality level so that I have the option later to use the clips in other projects.

The video file size note on this window says that each minute of video saved will consume 178MB of hard drive space. The finished two-minute video will therefore use at least 376MB of space. The Capture wizard also tells me that there is more than 34GB of available space on the hard drive that was selected, which is plenty of space to store extra video.

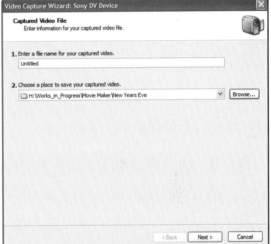

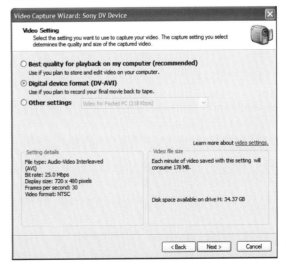

Manual capture

For the capture method, I opt to Capture parts of the tape manually. There is more on each tape than the footage from New Years Eve, and, for this session, I only want that selected footage.

By using the Capture Video window, I control the camcorder with the video recorder-style controls and leave the camcorder alone, not touching it at all during the capture process.

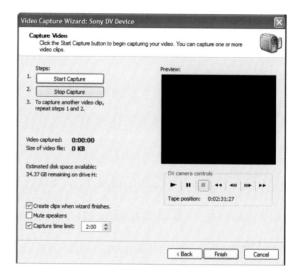

The tape position is shown as 0:02:31:27 (zero hours, 2 minutes, 31 seconds, and 27 frames into the tape). The computer knows the exact frame on the tape from the timestamp, which is embedded in the video signal by the camcorder during the shooting session. It took a couple minutes for the camcorder to rewind the tape to the beginning.

I then use the Play and Pause buttons to preview the video on the computer and camcorder to determine which video segments to capture. You can see the selection play on the computer monitor and, if you have an LCD monitor on the camcorder, you can see it there, too. You hear the audio only on the camcorder's speaker, but if you can see the video on the computer, the audio is being captured along with it.

Having found what I want to use, I usually add a second to the front and end of the footage, just in case the camcorder or computer needs a "running start" before the segment or a little "coast-down" time after it. A little extra at this step might save you from regretting not having a few more frames to use during editing.

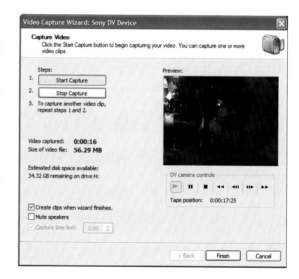

I don't turn off other software during a capture session—like virus protection, e-mail, and instant messaging applications. I was cautious at first, but as you gain experience with your setup and capturing results go smoothly, you will learn what things may effect capturing and which things will not. Capturing video from the camcorder to the computer seems to use less computer resources than transferring video from the computer back to the camcorder.

I captured the video on the digital camcorder tape in one segment. Up until you select Finish, Movie Maker uses temporary files, which are erased if you cancel the process.

After capturing two parts of the digital tape, Movie Maker created thumbnails for the clips and placed them in a single new collection folder. One 545MB DV-AVI file had been created.

I checked the two clips by previewing them a little to verify that they played back smoothly. Everything looked fine. The capture session with the digital tape was complete, and I switched the camera off.

Capture from analog tape

When I put the Hi8 analog tape into my digital camcorder and switched the camera back to the VCR position, the Video Capture wizard opened again. The control of the camcorder is the same as it was with the digital tape, with one exception: the tape position information isn't included. The frame information embedded in a digital camcorder recording is not present in an analog recording.

The DV-AVI file made from the analog camcorder tape was 13.7GB large and Movie Maker did not automatically create individual clips from it. I'll have to do it manually, something I often prefer to do to get to know each clip better and to cut the clips closer to where I want them.

The rest of the process for the analog tape was the same as it had been for the digital one. Previewing the file in Movie Maker showed that the DV-AVI file played smoothly, and the capture session was complete.

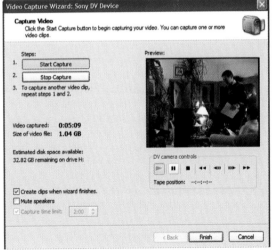

Arranging the collections tree

Clicking on the Collections button on the toolbar shows you the folder structure for working in Movie Maker. New folders were created automatically by the capture sessions, but I wanted to fine-tune the structure to one that would better facilitate the editing sessions.

To organize the folders better, I created a new folder named Movie Maker 2—Zero to Hero and dragged and dropped the new folder for my project into it.

When Movie Maker was closed and reopened, I noticed that the two new folders were about two-thirds of the way down a pretty big tree, so I decided to move them up to the top.

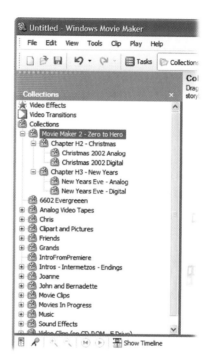

> With items sorted alphabetically, adding a leading space to the beginning of a folder name is enough to move it up into first place for future sessions.

Music for the background

The cut version of "Auld Lang Syne" was already a thumbnail in my Collections bin in one of the music folders, so I copied and pasted it from there to the new project folder. By copying the thumbnail, it remains in its original music folder for future use, and my changes to the music clip in the project won't affect its use for other purposes.

If it hadn't already been in my Movie Maker Collections folder but was on my computer, I could have imported it by choosing File > Import. If it was still on an audio CD, I'd have had to use another program like Windows Media Player to copy it to the computer.

Importing digital still pictures

Our digital still pictures of the New Year's get-together were not in my Collections folders. I only needed a few for the movie, so I reviewed them prior to importing and imported only those that would be real candidates. Forty-two still made the cut, with the potential of being used in the movie.

Before importing them, I created a new Collection subfolder as thumbnails because, unlike video clips where a new folder is created for each file imported, still pictures are added to the folder that is selected.

Sizes and file types of digital still pictures vary from camera to camera. These were from a 3.1-mega pixel camera and in JPG format with sizes of 1440x2160 pixels.

If the pictures are used without cropping or resizing, they will be automatically resized by Movie Maker to fit the video screen, with some black on the sides or the top and bottom. Not knowing which ones will be used in the final movie, it was too soon to crop or resize them.

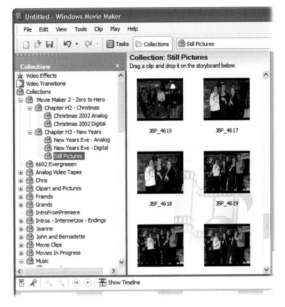

Splitting the analog video into clips

Movie Maker does not automatically create clips from the 38-minute video file captured from the analog camcorder tape.

The first thing I do when cropping a large clip is to make a copy of it so I can feel free to discard any of the smaller clips and get another copy, if needed, by going back to the original. First select the clip and then use CTRL-C to copy it to the clipboard, followed by CTRL-V to paste it into the folder as a duplicate.

The first round of clipping is just to break the single large video into individual scenes without regard to content (unless it's obviously garbage). I play the clip and pause it just past the transition point between scenes. Then, clicking the Split button under the monitor cuts the selected clip into two parts, the part before the cut and the part after.

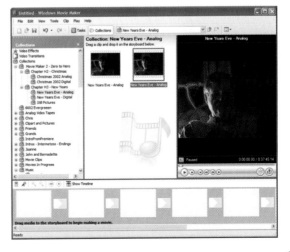

Movie Maker does a good job of splitting the clips as long as you pause just past the actual transition point, not before it.

I use the keyboard shortcut key F2 a lot during clip splitting, renaming the clips as I go. For this first pass, I give them sequential numbers and get to know them a little. This is the first time that I've taken a good look at each scene, beyond a casual passing glance. As I watch each scene, it's pretty easy to start mentally throwing away those that I don't want. But I leave them all in case I change my mind.

Clips for 25 individual scenes were made for the file from the analog tape.

Initial clip selection

With all the video clips now split into individual scenes, it is time for a more discerning review of all the clips from the digital and analog camcorders.

Movie Maker had created two clips for the video file from the digital tape. I looked at each to see if I wanted to change any of the split points or discard anything. They were darker than the clips from the analog camcorder, as I had expected. At this point, I was glad that I had opted to use both Hi8 and digital camcorders.

It is time to select the real candidates for the movie, split clips tighter, and discard unusable pieces. Each clip is given a descriptive name instead of a number.

Lots of splitting occurs during this review. A good example is a scene of each person in turn saying "Happy New Year." During the shooting, to avoid turning the camcorder on and off six times, it was left on and quick pans were done to go from person to person. It's time to clip out the panning, leaving a single clip of each person, which were definitely for the finished piece.

Creating a project by using the timeline

After lots of preparation, reviewing and thinking about each clip and still picture, and listening to the selected music piece a number of times, it's time to create a new project and start placing clips in it.

A new project starts when the first item is placed in the storyboard or timeline. Up until then, the clips and thumbnails are all individual items in the Collections folders and subfolders.

Many times, I find it is best to start with the music. You can only see the Audio/Music tracks when using the timeline view, so I toggle to that view. I drag the thumbnail of the music selection to the timeline and drop it in place. If it doesn't start at the beginning of the timeline, grab it and move it to the left until it does.

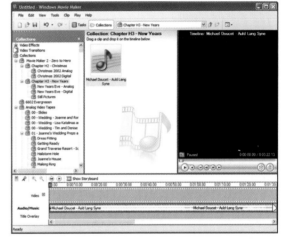

It's time to save the project and give it a name. It's a good habit to save a project early and keep resaving it every so often, especially if you make a major change that you're happy with. I leave the project file in the default folder so it'll be easier to find and open in the future.

Editing the music for length

The music clip didn't yet fit the allotted two-minute time frame; it was 3 minutes, 22 seconds long. Expanding the view of the timeline helps you see the patterns that the music makes. This helps considerably when actually doing the split. I play it a few times to determine where to split it and then zoom in on that spot and use the audio and visual feedback to make the actual split.

The music was slow and melancholy for the first minute and 22 seconds, and then it broke into a quick rhythmic Cajun-style beat for the next two minutes. The second part fits the time constraint and, as I wanted the movie to move along smartly, I picked the second part. I cut it where the first part trails off and the second part begins.

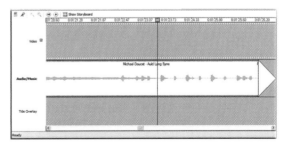

After the split, I selected and deleted the first part and dragged the second part to the left so that it begins at zero on the timeline.

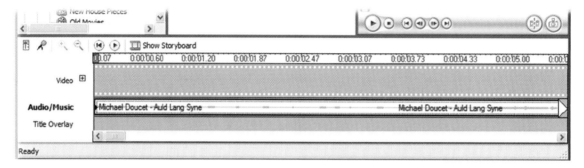

Additional still pictures

One great advantage of digital, nonlinear editing is that it's never too soon or too late to take in additional material, change your mind, and redo. Changes can easily be made all the way up to the moment of distributing the final movie. While I was working on the movie project, my wife was working with the still pictures we'd taken, brightening and enhancing them. I imported them into the appropriate project folder when they were ready.

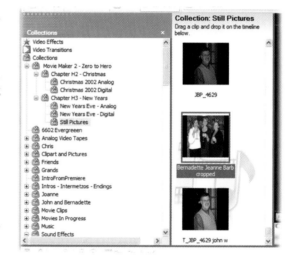

Storyboard and timeline views

At this point, I toggle to the storyboard view. During the editing process, I toggle between the timeline and storyboard views often. The storyboard view is where I add text, apply special effects to selected clips, and create transitions between clips.

Early in the editing process, I select the opening and closing clips. For the opening, I wanted to use clips that provide an overview of the setting. Toward or at the end, I wanted to use the six short clips that had each person saying "Happy New Year."

For the opening, I used a video clip of the table setting with a single flickering candle. Right-clicking the clip on the storyboard and selecting Fade In results in the clip fading in from a black background. The second clip completes the overview, a still picture that overviews the group.

To save a little time and to have the transition from the first to the second clip happen more in time with the music, I grab the still picture and slide it to the left to overlap the first clip by about two seconds. The overlap results in the two clips fading from one to the other, one of my favorite types of transitions.

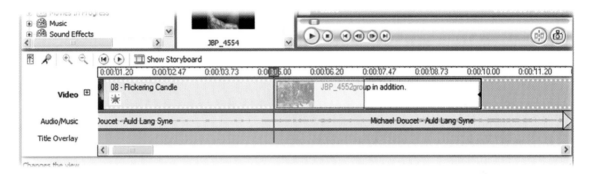

The opening titles

With 10 seconds on the timeline, a Title overlay is added to help introduce the movie. From the menu, choose Tools > Titles and Credits. With the first clip selected on the timeline, select "Title on the selected clip".

I entered New Year's Eve and 2003, selected the BroadwayComD font, made the transparency 25 percent, and enlarged the font by 5 times. I left the alignment as centered and finished it by applying the title to the timeline.

Then I stretched the title on the timeline by grabbing its right edge and pulling it to the right, until it went from the beginning of the first clip to covering most of the second clip as well.

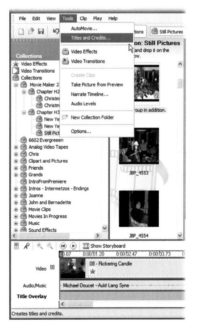

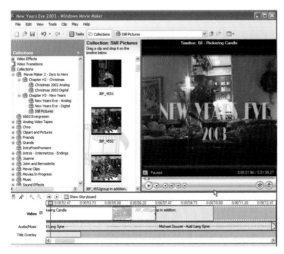

Editing decisions

With the music track in place and the opening clips and title in place, it's time to review the clips in the collection and determine which ones fit best in the movie and where. Do they fit the tempo of the music and the overall video?

Even within two minutes, I like to give a movie a beginning, middle, and end. The socializing earlier in the evening is the scene for the first half of the movie, and watching the countdown to midnight on TV makes for the second half. The clips of people saying "Happy New Year" were for the closing clips. I only had to select some more clips for the two halves and find a couple of nice clips to provide a midpoint transition. The midpoint is not fixed in time and, depending on the clips, the midpoint in terms of content might move. The clips themselves often tell you what works best.

Move some clips to the timeline and preview the movie to help you determine what should be added next. With such a short movie, you can watch it over and over many times. You just need some concept in mind of what you want to achieve. Nonlinear editing facilitates endless experimenting. Do something, watch it, change it—over and over until your concept emerges into reality. One approach is to preview the movie and note which parts are the worst. Change those and note the next worst. Do this over and over until it gets so hard to find a bad part that you call it "finished."

Closing titles

Now I added the closing credits, overlaying the final picture with the names of the couples and "Happy New Year," using scrolling credits. I used the same font as I did for the title text—BroadwayComD, with the transparency setting at 25 percent. However, this time I didn't increase the font size. I left the alignment as centered.

Placing text over a clip is a great experience—there are so many choices and Movie Maker previews each choice so well. I select Fade, Wipe and apply it. Additionally, I fade out the final picture so it goes to black as the movie ends.

Sending as an e-mail attachment

The default setting for an e-mail attachment is a maximum file size of 1MB, just what we've decided to use. You can use Tools > Options and use the Advanced tab to change this size, increasing it in 1MB increments to a maximum of 10MB.

In Movie Maker, with the project open, click the Tasks button and choose Finish Movie > Send in e-mail. This starts the Save Movie wizard.

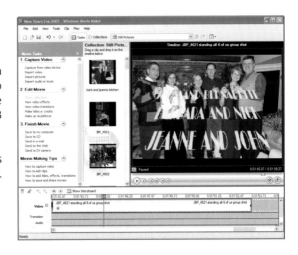

The Save Movie wizard shows the progress of the movie being saved. It took about 10 minutes to render this two-minute movie. Movie Maker will make the best video file that it can within the constraint you give it, in this case, a file size of 1MB.

The Save Movie wizard then gives you options to play the rendered movie in your Windows Media Player (a good idea to check) and save a copy of it on your computer before sending it out. If you save a copy of the movie, you can select the location and name for the saved movie. When finished with this window, click the Next button to create the e-mail in your default e-mail software.

In your e-mail, add a personal note (and remember your audience's address!). Movie Maker includes a message in your e-mail that provides the receivers with a link to use if they need to upgrade their Windows Media Player to view the movie.

Click Send and that's it, your e-mail movie postcard will be winging its way to your friends—and I'm sure they'll be impressed.

A final word

During digital video work, you will probably run into some computer-related issues that may frustrate you until you learn how to deal with them.

With computers, there are usually many different ways to accomplish the same thing, so no hurdle should be considered a dead end—just a learning challenge or opportunity. If you need some help with resolving camera, computer, software, and Internet issues, try the forums at www.friendsofed.com or the microsoft.public.windowsxp.moviemaker newsgroup (at www.microsoft.com) as a resource—I'll see you there! Have fun and enjoy many rewarding experiences making digital movies.

Editing a vacation movie

John Buechler

In this chapter's project, the vacation is a trip that was made from Vancouver, Canada passing through Saskatchewan and ending up in Toronto. But whatever your vacation may be, it probably has a particularly well-defined progression of events—and thus provides a very clear storyline. Therefore, planning the storyboard for your video and how you are going to execute the design are factors you have to consider before you piece the project together.

Movie Maker 2 is an easy program to edit your footage in—which allows you to pay more attention to the creative process.

We will begin by planning the movie that is centred on a trip traveling across Canada. We will consider all areas of the project from the initial idea to planning and storyboarding the project, creating it in Movie Maker, and finally outputting it to DV tape. This chapter will cover the following:

- ★ Checking your settings
- ★ Designing a movie
- ★ Planning your vacation movie
- ★ Gathering your materials, capturing several clips, and importing still images
- ★ Organizing your footage within a collection
- ★ Drawing a storyboard on paper
- ★ Editing your movie by following the storyboard
- ★ Adding transitions and video effects
- ★ Outputting the movie to a DV tape

Why output to a DV tape?

Why would you spend time recording your movie back to a video cassette? The main reason is that you can hook up your DV camera to a television or a video recorder and watch your movies on a larger screen or tape them for someone with a VCR.

Outputting your movie to DV tape also is beneficial for several other reasons.

You can maintain a high-quality version of your movie without taking up space on your hard drive. Backing up your projects on DV tape is a low-cost alternative to storing your movies on a hard drive while maintaining quality.

DV allows **loss-less digitization**: transferring it back to your computer will not mean you will lose quality during transmission.

In the UK and Europe, some consumer digital video cameras have the DV-In socket disabled; this is due to complex tax laws regarding recording television programs. They can be modified by experienced electronics experts or by adding so-called "widgets," but this will void any warranty.

Planning a vacation movie

There are many different kinds of vacation movies, primarily because of different locations, seasons, weather, and of course, purpose. Your vacation movie might take place at an amusement park or be a family celebration like Christmas or an educational trip. In any event, it is important to match the graphics, effects, and text you use when editing your movie to the kind of vacation.

Making these kinds of decisions is part of the planning stage—where you gather what you are going to use and think about how you are going to edit it by using Movie Maker. The planning stage is vital before starting your footage collection and building your movie, if you're going to be working with such a large amount of footage. This means that before we get started, you should consider the following questions:

★ What is the theme or purpose of the vacation movie, and how will your editing reflect this?

★ What footage should you capture, and is it relevant to the story?

★ Where is your footage coming from—video or stills?

★ What kind of audio are you going to use? Music and/or narration?

★ How much footage can you capture?

★ How should this footage be ordered in the movie?

So let's consider what we intend to produce and then the materials that we have available for our project. We have video footage of all three locations (Vancouver, Saskatchewan, and Toronto), including plane travel. We also have photographic stills of two of those locations: Vancouver and Toronto. We will capture some stills from the video footage to add to the movie project and narrate an audio track onto the timeline.

Once we've figured out what we need for our project, we can make a list of them:

★ Video footage from two DV tapes
★ Stills from hard drive
★ Microphone to narrate audio track

This step, for a smaller project such as this, can usually be skipped. However, if you have a complicated project, sometimes it helps to organize your source files and make a list of what you are going to use and where you are going to get it from.

Making movies about vacations

The fortunate aspect about movies about vacations is that they usually have a well-defined sequence of events. In most cases, you will probably want to follow an established timeline, which is probably already laid out on the DV tapes for you! It is much easier than other forms of events, where the footage may not be taken in the order you want to edit it in Movie Maker. We will talk more about sequencing your footage later in the section about storyboarding.

All footage is not created equal

At this point, you will want to review your footage for what will be useful and what will not be usable. Review which footage might be too shaky to use, clips that are too short, or perhaps areas of the video that are of poor lighting or quality. With vacation videos, probably mostly shot "handheld style" while you were enjoying yourself, it's very easy to end up with a large amount of unusable footage. Given that, and depending on quality, the more footage you have, the better off you are.

Most of the decisions made about what footage to use is left up to common sense, aesthetics, and the needs of your individual project.

Generally speaking, dark and muddy, pixel-laden/blocky, blurry, and shaky images are not well liked. As you can see, the picture of the cat, here, is dark (which is not favorable for the subject), blurry, green—and, if you were to watch it, also incredibly shaky.

Clear, well-lit, and stable shots are usually successful in a project. As you can see, there is contrast and lighting in the footage of the snowy landscape. This video is also much more stable (if you were to watch it) and clear. It might not be great footage, but it is certainly a lot better and adequate for our movie.

After reviewing the amount of footage you have that is worthwhile, you will want to start constructing the story you want to tell. This is when sketching out your ideas on paper in a storyboard format might be useful.

You might want to also wait until you capture your footage into Movie Maker before organizing your thoughts onto paper. For this project, we are going to create a storyboard on paper after collecting and capturing the source files.

If you have a lot of footage and you are unsure about what you want to capture onto your hard drive, I advise that you draft a storyboard at this point instead of later on. That way, you can follow along and capture only what you need for your video project when you get to that stage.

If you have a lot of footage, skip ahead and read **Making a storyboard by hand**, *and organize your thoughts before you start capturing.*

If you don't have much footage, it might be easier to capture your video clips first and then use the thumbnail images in Movie Maker as a basis to organize your thoughts into a storyboard.

Setting up Movie Maker 2 for a project

Open Movie Maker. The first thing we'll do is check the current settings and make sure they are right for this project. There are many different options you can control in Movie Maker. In this particular project, we want to pay particular attention to these settings before getting started.

General settings

First of all, check the general settings. To open the dialog box, go to Tools > Options. The Options dialog box will open. Click on the General tab. The dialog box will now look similar to this one shown. Just how similar will depend on your desktop theme.

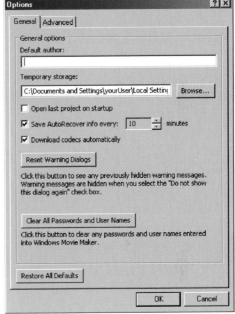

Save AutoRecover info

You might want to decrease or increase this setting based on the capabilities of your computer. If you have problems with Movie Maker 2 crashing, you may

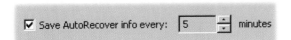

want to ensure that this setting is a short interval so that you don't lose your project information.

We will change this setting so that Movie Maker saves AutoRecover information every five minutes. This feature saved me many times during the creation of this particular project.

Always remember the golden rule of computing: save early, save often.

Temporary storage

This is an important setting to consider when you are planning to create movies that are particularly large. Before Movie Maker records your movie to DV tape (during output), a temporary file is created and stored at the location specified in this dialog box.

If the drive that you choose for this location has a **FAT32** file system, then you will encounter problems if your temporary video file becomes larger than 4GB. FAT32 systems do not allow file sizes greater than 4GB, which is possible to exceed if you are creating a large video.

If you are working with particularly long videos, then you will need to set your Temporary storage place to a NTFS drive, or create a shorter video.

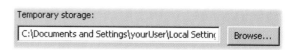

So how do you find out how big your video is? Open Windows Explorer (WINDOWS+E) and find the drive you want to save your temporary file to. Right-click on its icon and choose Properties and the Disk Properties dialog box will open:

You can see the File System: in this dialog box.

> For more information on formatting your partitions and file systems, see this web site: www.microsoft.com/WINDOWSXP/home/using/ productdoc/en/choosing_between_NTFS_FAT_a nd_FAT32.asp

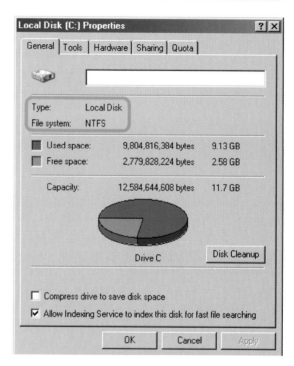

When you're happy with your settings in this box, click OK.

Advanced settings

Back in Movie Maker, we'll also work with the Advanced settings. Open the Options dialog box by choosing Tools > Options. Then, click on the Advanced tab. The dialog box will look somewhat similar to this.

You will also need to set the default Picture duration for the still images you are going to import for your video.

When you place your picture stills in the storyboard/timeline, the duration you set here will be for how long they appear. For this project, we are going to set our default duration to three seconds. We'll have to alter the duration of some images individually, but most will sit well with the pace of the video at three seconds.

You can also set the default Transition duration in the Advanced settings. This will set the amount of time the transition between video clips on the timeline/storyboard in your movie project will take.

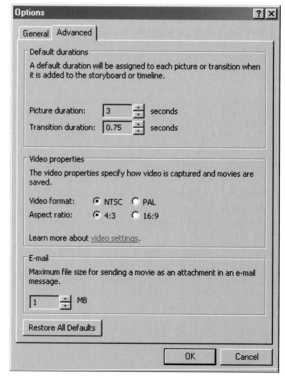

Use the up and down arrow buttons to scroll through the available time lengths. For this project, we've set the default Transition duration to a short 0.75 seconds. We can change individual transition lengths later, but no complex transitions are planned for this movie—just simple fades—and that will be long enough.

Video format and aspect ratio

The format of your movie is going to depend on what kind of camera you are using, which varies depending on your location. **NTSC** format is found in Canada, USA, and Japan, whereas **PAL** format is found in Europe, the UK, and parts of South America. Because the camera being used for this project is a North American model, we are using NTSC.

The aspect ratios are 16:9 for widescreen and 4:3 for normal television. Because the video footage wasn't shot with widescreen in mind, 4:3 is the setting we'll choose.

Video format:	⦿ NTSC	○ PAL
Aspect ratio:	⦿ 4:3	○ 16:9

Gathering your footage for capture

Now that your settings are in order, it is time to start gathering your footage, image stills, or audio clips into a Movie Maker collection.

Capturing from the DV

The first thing you want to do is make sure that you have enough room on your hard drive to capture the footage you need for your movie. All video varies in size, but you will want to allow approximately a couple hundred megabytes of hard drive space for each minute of video that you capture. If you are capturing video by using different software and then importing your videos into Movie Maker, this number can be far greater (sometimes up to 1GB per minute).

Create a new project (File > New Project) if you haven't already.

Make sure that your camera is in VCR/VTR or playback mode and that it's hooked up by a FireWire (IEEE-1394) cable to your computer.

Go to the Movie Tasks pane, and under the Capture Video heading, click on Capture from video device. For this first step, we are going to capture our Vancouver footage into a collection.

Make sure that your video camera is plugged in to your computer, and the **Video Capture Wizard** will start.

The first window in the Video Capture wizard prompts you to enter a file name for the captured video files. Here we have typed "vancouver" into the text field. This will create our Vancouver collection. Later we'll add some still photos to this collection.

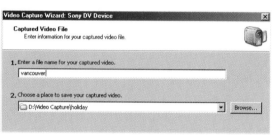

Then browse to an area on your computer where you want your captured video files to be stored. Make sure you have enough room on the chosen drive to save your video files. When you're finished with the dialog box, click on the Next button.

In the next step, select the setting used to capture video. This dialog box is where you tell Movie Maker the size and quality of video to capture. Because we are outputting back to a DV tape, we need to select the second option, Digital device format (DV-AVI).

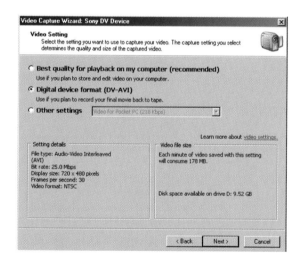

You can look at the setting details area of this dialog box for more information on how Movie Maker captures your video. As you can see here, the quality is higher and suited to how we are going to output the movie later.

After you have chosen your video setting, click on the Next button.

The next dialog box, called Capture Method, is where we can choose how to capture the video. In this project, we are going to capture different parts of the video manually. We want to pick and choose which clips we need to tell the story, so we'll need to select Show preview during capture.

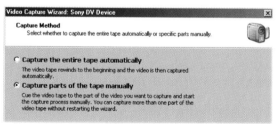

After you have chosen your capture method, click on the Next button.

Now the fun part—capturing the footage!

The first tape we have has footage from Vancouver. Watch through the tape, and press the Start Capture button as necessary to gather your clips and Stop Capture when you're finished. Repeat as necessary until you have all your footage from this city.

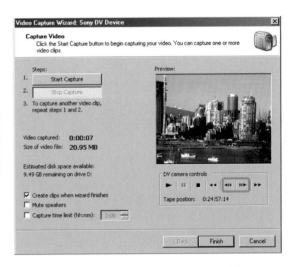

> Remember that you can use the frame-by-frame controls (highlighted) to choose accurately where to begin grabbing your clips.

When you are finished, click on Finish. Then, Movie Maker will create a clip of the selected footage you have gathered and add a new video into your collection.

Rename this clip as necessary. Then, repeat these steps for each city (or major section or part) of your vacation. In our project, we have created a collection for vancouver, saskatoon, toronto, and flights. These will help us organize each different area so it will be a lot easier to compose and edit our movie later on.

vancouver

Importing your stills

On their holidays, many people also take along a digital or 35mm camera to take still photos. You can and will probably want to import a few of these images to incorporate into the movie as well. If they are not from a digital camera, you will have to scan them in. In any event, they will have to be on your computer, as image files, already—Movie Maker itself does not capture from still image devices.

When choosing your photos, you want to make sure that they are relevant to the storyline and flow well with the footage. If your photos contrast greatly in color, size, or brightness, they might stick out too much from the rest of your video clips. If it is difficult to tell, sometimes the best way to find this out is by trial and error.

Select the collection you want to add pictures into. First, we are going to add pictures to the vancouver collection.

If it's not open already, open the movie tasks pane by clicking on the Tasks button. From that, select Import Pictures, and the Import File dialog box will open.

Browse through your image files and select pictures that you plan to use in your movie, pressing the CTRL key to choose more than one, and click on the Import button. After you have chosen the files, they are automatically added to the open collection. You can rename the pictures, if you like, in the collections pane.

Repeat this as necessary for your other collections.

Organizing your source files

Now that you have successfully imported and captured all your source files into collections in Movie Maker, it is time to start organizing everything into a logical order.

This is where a storyboard becomes useful, in that it will help you design a movie that is coherent and interesting. You will probably find that you come up with a lot of ideas.

Making a storyboard by hand

Storyboards can be vastly complex or very simple processes. Movie Maker has a storyboard in its very own framework—and for simple movies, it's a more than adequate organizational tool.

If your video is very short or you already have a very clear idea of what you intend to do, you might skip this step or do it entirely in Movie Maker. However, getting your ideas down on paper can be very helpful. Many people, from painters to web designers, sketch ideas on paper before beginning production. Creating a storyboard for your movie is a good way to start your project.

It will depend on your subject and your source files how you do this—but we are going to break down the trip into smaller sections to deal with first:

- ★ Vancouver (leaving)
- ★ Flight
- ★ Saskatoon
- ★ Flight

★ Toronto
★ Flight
★ Vancouver (returning)

For most of these areas, we are going to storyboard each major transition in the form of a brief sketch. Mercifully, it's not necessary to be an artist to do a usable storyboard; a storyboard consisting of stick figures and blocks will work equally well.

Also, if you are creating enough storyboard pictures, you might want to add some captions at this stage. This will help you plan and remember what you want your captions to say at each major point in the movie. Write brief descriptions below the clips if you feel you need to—it can help.

The reason we did this step after capturing our footage is because there was comparatively little footage to capture, and it was very clear what we would be using for our vacation footage. In other words, almost all footage taken was also captured and then used.

Also, it was helpful to have the short clips to "scrub" through (manually move the timeline's playhead to watch the footage) in order to develop the story.

The more footage you take, the better your movie will be! Strive to take as much footage as possible, and then carefully choose clips to capture onto your computer before even starting Movie Maker. A great way to help in this process is by sketching out storyboards.

Drafting a narration script

Roughing out a script at this stage is also a good idea. You have your footage and a good idea of how that footage is going to go in your movie. You do not necessarily want to write the entire script word for word, but you will certainly want to get an idea of what you need to communicate in your movie, which will help you edit it.

Draft a rough script, and in the following section, you can finalize it after you know the length of your movie and each clip.

If you have a time limit for your movie already, it can help to do a rough draft of the script first. I generally work on a script being read at three words per second.

Editing the vacation movie

Now it is time to start editing the movie. In this section, we will add the video clips and stills to the project and then add audio, effects, and transitions to form the final movie.

Following your storyboard

If you are creating a movie of your vacation in a similar order to the progression of this chapter, you will have sketched a storyboard for the project. Having a storyboard drawn makes it very easy for you to start dragging and dropping your video clips onto the Movie Maker storyboard and then to trim the footage as needed on the timeline.

Even though your Movie Maker storyboard will not look the same as the one you drew earlier, the general flow of events will end up being similar when you play the movie preview. Your hand-drawn storyboard is a tool to remind you of ideas, captioning, and the general flow of your project.

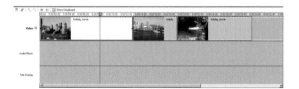

By using the start and end trim handles, you can accurately edit and reuse your video clips in the timeline view. By organizing the entire set of source files into several different collections based on each city or event, it is possible to add quickly source files to the timeline based on the storyboard we drew earlier.

Adding transitions to the vacation movie

Transitions are an important part of many movies. They help each video clip flow from one to another. Transitions, such as cross-fades (called Fade in the Video Transitions collection) and dissolves, combine two clips so that they blur or "run into" one another.

Transitions can easily enhance, but equally detract, from the overall feel of your production. If you use too many very obvious and apparent transitions, they can interrupt the flow of your movie.

Carefully choose which transitions you want to use, and don't use too many different transitions! Try to choose a few that will either tie in with the feeling or theme of your movie or subtly enhance the overall quality.

Because many of the video clips used in this movie are short, it is more effective to choose transitions that are short and subtle. At the beginning of the chapter, we set transitions to a very short duration (0.75 seconds). We are also using a simple Fade for most of the transitions.

Drag your chosen transitions between clips on the storyboard/timeline. The transitions are depicted pictorially in the timeline view, with clips overlaid and faded into one another.

Watch a transition frame by frame in the preview monitor or scrub slowly across it on the timeline. This can help you easily see what you have edited and decide what clips require transitions and, if they do, which ones work best.

Here two different video clips, of the view from a plane and a shot of one of the vacation destinations, are cross-fading. This helps give a sense of flow between the two very different video clips.

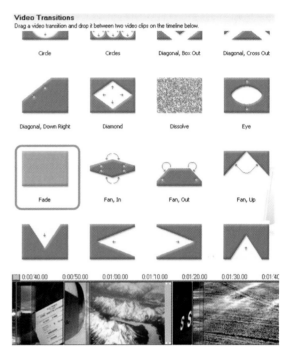

Adding effects to clips

Adding effects is done in a very similar way to transitions, and we can also apply some of the same considerations for using them. Too many effects, or too many different effects, can detract from almost any movie. A great number of effects are distracting to your audience. This can cause them to pay too much attention to the effects and not enough to your story, narration, or videography.

However, some of the effects in Movie Maker are useful and, when used carefully, can add a great deal of quality to your footage. Sometimes, using the same effect across all your clips will work well. Even using a combination of two different effects can look particularly interesting and unique.

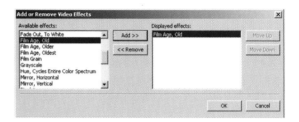

Drag effects to clips from the Video Effects collection, or right-click on a clip and use the Add or Remove Video Effects dialog box.

Test different effects and combinations with your footage, as the footage will all react in slightly different ways, depending on its composition.

On this shot of the Toronto skyline, the Film Age, Old effect is used to add some graininess to the footage, giving it perceived age. Does it work? Well, take a look for yourself! (It looks better in motion, by the way.)

Reading the script, adding narration

Our video is quite bland without a narration. If you watched this particular vacation movie, you would not have much of an idea of what is going on—where we were or which parts were shot in each place—and that would make it rather boring to watch. Our narration should explain what the audience is watching and what is happening in the progression of events.

Watch through your movie, and create a script that is specifically timed to the series of video clips. Pay careful attention to transitions between the scenes and how long you have for each part. You will obviously need to run through the movie a couple times so you have an idea about timing and how much you will be able to narrate. Remember that you don't have to do it all in one go—you can start and stop your voice capture at any time.

When you are ready, click on the Narrate Timeline button. After clicking on the icon, you will see the following pane, where you can start and stop the recording process. Connect a microphone to your computer, and, once it is hooked up and turned on, the Input level meter should light up automatically.

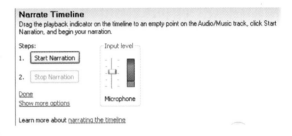

Make sure that you watch the input level closely as you record your voice. Do a test first, speaking into the microphone and watching the meter. If the meter tends to lean toward the red end of the scale, it means you will probably have a lot of **clipping** in your narration—losing parts of it. If this is the case, lower the input level until the meter is typically in the upper green- to yellow-level range.

Capture your narration for the movie by moving the playhead to an empty spot on the Audio/Music layer. Click on the Start Narration button, and start speaking into the microphone.

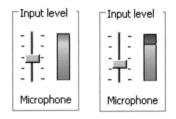

As soon as you click on Stop Narration, Movie Maker will prompt you to name the audio clip. Then it will import the file and place it on the Audio/Music layer.

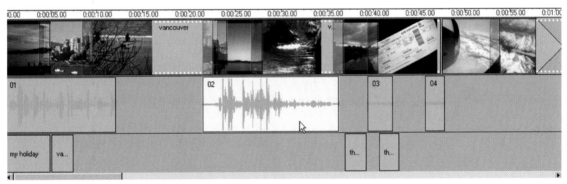

After you have finished adding your narration, listen to what you have just produced. Now you might discover that you need to change the audio level balance between the Audio layer (the audio imported with your video clips) and the narration you just added. If there is little contrast between the two different audio tracks, it will be very difficult for your audience to hear.

Click on the Set Audio Levels icon:

The Audio Levels dialog box will open. This is where you can set the balance between the two different sources of audio. In our project, we are going to make the audio on the Audio/Music layer more prominent because it is a narration. However, if you need to hear the audio coming from the DV tape source files and are adding a background music layer, you would then want the opposite.

Adding captions and titles

After you have put together your timeline full of video clips and images, we can lay down titles and captions for the movie. It is a good idea to leave this step to last because if you move, edit, or add certain effects to your movie, then your captions might all of a sudden be in the wrong place.

For the captions, you will want to select the clip to caption and then select Make titles or credits. The captions in our project are mainly overlaying certain clips on the timeline, which means we need to select the clips and then use the Add title on the selected clip option.

Hopefully, through storyboarding or preplanning, you have an idea of what you need to do for this step. For our movie, we are going to keep it relatively simple.

Because our vacation is not quite fun enough for a Comic Sans-type font, nor romantic enough for a scripty-font, we shall keep everything clean and simple with a clean and classic Verdana font. In other words, try to choose a font that somewhat matches your vacation.

As you can see, we are choosing a subtitle overlay as our title animation. This is so we can see more and take advantage of the picture we are overlaying the title on.

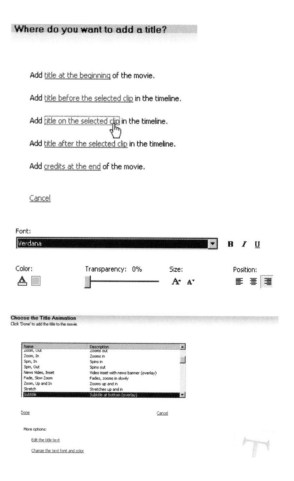

The Title Overlay layer allows you to layer titles or animated titles on top of video or still images, and we can trim the title to be the same length as our still image on the Video layer.

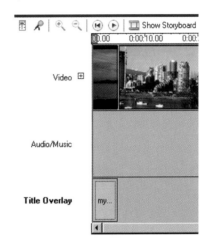

As you can see, keeping it simple can be very effective. However, if you have a less active background image or video, you might want to add some fancier fonts or more animation.

If you are using text on your Video layer (perhaps on a still image titled in Adobe Photoshop and imported), try to keep your words inside the title safe area—a few inches in from all edges of the screen. Graphics placed outside the safe area may not display properly on a television screen.

Continue through your footage and follow your storyboards, adding titles or captions onto the Title Overlay layer. Open the timeline view and select a still image or video clip to which you want to add a caption.

> Remember that if you add your titles and then you edit the progression of your footage again, you will also need to move your captions to match the correct video clip or image.

Output your movie to a DV tape

You have finished organizing your timeline, adding transitions and effects, recording a narration, and adding titles and captions to your Movie Maker project, therefore you are ready to output your movie to DV tape! This section will show you all the steps we went through in successfully taping the movie back onto a DV tape in your video camera.

A couple of things you will want to think about before outputting your movie follows:

★ Do you have enough room on the tape?
★ Will your camcorder be ready, or does it need a few seconds to wind up at the start of the recording process?

If you do not have enough room to tape your movie, you can change the format of your tape from **SP** to **LP**. This setting can be changed in or on your video camcorder.

You might also run into problems if your DV camcorder does not start quickly enough when recording the movie. This means that the beginning of your movie will not make it to the tape. Movie Maker will prompt you with an error message, alerting you about this problem.

What you need to do is create a plain "image" in any graphics editor. Save this image and import it back into Movie Maker. Drop this at the beginning of your movie and edit it so that it appears for a few seconds to compensate for the dropped frames.

Using the Save Movie wizard

First of all, to record onto a DV video camcorder, you will need to make sure that your camera is in either **VCR**, **VTR**, or **playback mode**. Which mode it is in depends on your particular brand or model of camcorder. It should look similar to this:

If you are lucky, you might even have more than one camera connected to your computer! If so, Movie Maker will ask you to choose which one of these cameras has the DV tape you want to record to. If you only have one camera, you will not be given the option.

Start the Save Movie wizard by clicking on Send to DV Camera in the tasks pane.

The Save Movie wizard begins by prompting you to fast-forward or rewind the DV tape to the point where you want to begin recording your movie. You should be very cautious when cueing your DV tape at this point.

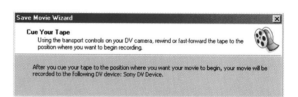

Make sure you check the length of your movie and that you have enough tape available so that you will not end up overwriting (taping over) any existing footage or any footage that you want to keep.

You can use the controls on your DV camera to cue the tape. Click on Next when you are ready.

After clicking on Next, you will see a warning saying "The content of your will tape be overwritten and lost." Double check that your tape is cued to the right position, and click on Yes.

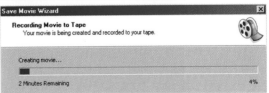

The movie you have created will begin saving and recording onto the DV tape in your camcorder. The Recording Movie to Tape dialog box will depict the process of your movie being recorded.

Before Movie Maker starts recording to your tape, a temporary file will be made on your hard drive. You set the location of this file in your General settings earlier in this chapter. Remember that there is a limited file size depending on the configuration of your computer system.

You can watch your DV camera while the movie is being recorded to the tape. The display on your camcorder, if it has one, will display the time on the tape as it is being recorded.

After the movie has finished being recorded to the tape, the temporary file that was created in the process will be deleted from your hard drive. And that is it!

A new dialog box appears when your movie has finished taping. Simply click on the Finish button to close the dialog box.

Troubleshooting the output process

You could very well run into problems during this process; connecting differing types of hardware to your computer can be a complex business. Let's look at a few of the things you might run into during this process and what you can do to fix or avoid the following problems:

★ No DV device found or No tape in DV camera Your camera might be turned off or not connected to the computer. Also, the camera might be in standby mode (some cameras automatically enter this mode). Check your connections and camera mode, and then try again.

If your camera enters standby mode, try removing the battery and plugging it in by using your camera's AC adapter. Many models will not enter standby mode when powered this way.

- ★ DV tape is write protected—Make sure that the tape is in the record position.

- ★ Switch camera to VCR mode—Your camera might not be in VCR/VTR or playback mode. Switch the camera into this mode, or turn off the camera entirely, and then switch it into VCR mode.

Watching your taped movie

When you are finished, try hooking your DV camera to a television set to see how your movie turned out.

You will notice that the brightness of your footage against what you see on the computer screen varies greatly.

Your video footage on the computer monitor is probably quite a bit darker than it looks on video. You will notice that, back on the video tape, it will go back to looking nice and bright again!

If you've been following along with your own footage, you should now have a professional-looking, documentary-style movie all about a vacation or trip. Not only that, but by virtue of being recorded on DV tape, you can impress your friends by showing it on their TVs—or, by using a video recorder, make copies and send it out to people.

We have covered many different topics while learning how to prepare your footage, edit, and output a movie based on a vacation. By looking at techniques such as storyboarding, making lists, and organizing source files, you learned how to prepare a production so that you can save time editing.

During the editing process, you learned how to use the storyboards to execute your production in a logical manner and to use transitions and effects to enhance (not detract from!) productions.

Finally, you output this movie to DV tape and considered ways to avoid errors, and what to do if you encountered them. All you need to do now is rummage through all those old vacation tapes you've got and edit the lot!

> *If you're planning to make VHS copies, it's a good idea to put 10 to 20 seconds of black screen lead-in time before your masterpiece because VCRs often take a few seconds to track to the tape properly.*

Videotaping an event

John Buechler

In this chapter

In this chapter, we'll use Movie Maker 2 to make a 15-minute movie that uses camcorder video tapes and digital still pictures. We'll cover the processes in Movie Maker thoroughly and cover using other software needed to make a video CD (VCD), a super video CD (SVCD), or a DVD from the movie file saved by Movie Maker.

I'm going to use footage from a family outing at Saugatuck, a resort town on the shore of Lake Michigan. We'll capture the camcorder footage, import the digital still pictures, create and edit the movie, and then save it in two different formats that are suitable for viewing as a high-quality movie on TV, with a DVD player or a specialized VCD player.

This chapter will cover the following:

★ Capturing video from a camcorder
★ Arranging and reviewing captured video, making clips
★ Importing still pictures and music
★ Editing the movie project
★ Saving the movie on a VCD, SVCD, or DVD
★ Saving the movie onto a CD

Thinking about formats

During the process of making a 15-minute movie and recording it onto a CD or DVD, you may run into computer-related issues more so than those you would come across in making the two-minute movie in **Chapter H1**. Issues such as file sizes more than 2 or 4GB may require you to change your hard drive file system, obtain and learn other software needed to burn CDs or DVDs, or resolve issues with your CD or DVD burning software and hardware.

Also, the CD or DVD that you produce isn't necessarily going to play on the DVD players of your friends or family members. Issues with playing movies are mostly due to differences with hardware and software standards; they do not necessarily mean that something is wrong with the CD/DVD you give them or with their playback unit. The electronic world continues to move on apace and as time goes on, more and more equipment will be compatible.

Planning and preparation

The inspiration for this movie came months after the event occurred; the grayness and cold of the winter months inspired the summertime theme. With your new interest in digital movie editing and your personal collection of old videotapes, home movies, family picture albums, and the like, you will often want to create a movie from material that already exists, as opposed to planning and producing a new fully staged one.

Nonlinear editing (NLE) allows you to go into the editing process at any point, do however little or much you want, then go wherever else you want and do some more. You can start with making closing credits if you love that area, then move over to opening titles, and then put video and audio clips on the timeline. At any point, you can import more video footage or still pictures, change or delete anything already in the movie. You may skip around in your work; however, this chapter will cover the process in a more linear way.

Choosing music

I like to start with background music. With a 15-minute target, a number of different, but perhaps related, pieces will be needed. The video footage does not have the high action content that a soccer game might have, so slower, quieter pieces may be more appropriate. Think about the overall theme of the movie as you browse your music library. Another approach for background audio would be to use some of the camcorder footage with lapping waves and seagulls.

Hard drive space

For a 15-minute movie of DVD quality, you should have lots of free hard drive space on a recently defragged hard drive before starting the project, and defrag often during it. A 15-minute DVD quality video will itself take around 4GB uncompressed, so to help the software run smoothly, 10GB is a more realistic figure.

Sources of extra footage

Although, for this movie, the event had passed months earlier, it isn't too late to obtain additional video footage or still pictures to include in the project. Others at the event may have taken video or pictures that you can get. If you found a shell or something else on the beach and brought it home, you can scan it or take a picture to include. There are many ways to get digital inputs for a project. Use your creativity as you round up the potential source clips.

Capturing video from the camcorder

I had video footage on two different camcorder tapes and digital still pictures from a couple different cameras. In total, there was more than an hour of camcorder tape footage and about 100 still pictures. With a lot of video and still material, look at the source material to see if the project will be mostly a video with some interspersed stills or a slide-show with interspersed video clips. In this case, my content seems to warrant making a video with some stills mixed in.

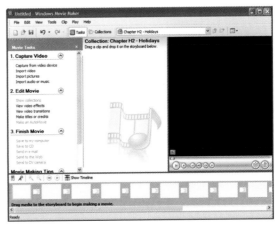

Having planned and thought about the project a bit, it's time to move into making it. The first thing we need to do is get all the source material into the computer and into Movie Maker. Connect the digital camcorder to the FireWire cable and, in Movie Maker, go to the Capture Video section of the tasks pane and select Capture from video device.

With a tape in the digital camcorder and the external power supply attached (to preclude any low-power situations during capture), turn the camcorder on to VCR mode.

The Video Capture wizard appears, asking for a file name and location. Fill in a name—in this case, Saugatuck—and chose your location. Verify the file name and location one last time and click Next to go to the Video Setting window.

In the Video Setting window, select the Digital device format (DV-AVI) if it's not already selected by default. This format will be of sufficiently high quality to make a DVD. Note that it says each minute of video will consume 178 MB, and there is 26.17GB available on the selected drive for this project. Click Next to go to the Capture Method window.

There is an awful lot of footage on the video tape, and it will be far easier to capture only sections we may want to use, so select Capture parts of the tape manually and click Next to go on to the Capture Video window.

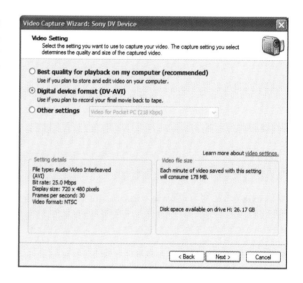

Manual capture from analog tapes

The tape containing the footage is analog Hi8 format, so no tape position is shown on the Capture Video window. Click the rewind button under the Preview: picture to rewind the tape to the beginning.

Open the camcorder LCD screen, if needed, so you can hear the video as it is captured. Watch the tape by using the on-screen controls. Use the Start Capture and Stop Capture buttons at the upper left as needed to capture the footage of interest.

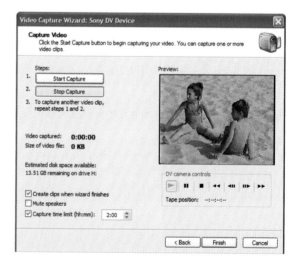

Each segment of the tape will be saved on your computer as a temporary file. When you're done with this tape, click the Finish button to have Movie Maker create the DV-AVI file for the tape in your desired folder. It will show you the importing progress window as the DV-AVI file is created.

Change tapes and repeat the capture process with the second tape. You will get a disconnect message each time you stop the camcorder.

> *If the video being captured seems a bit choppy, it's possible that the selected disk is getting full. Change to another drive before capturing the footage from the second tape, or clean up and defrag the hard drive again.*

When you've completed the capture process for all your tapes, return to the main Movie Maker window.

Arranging collections

Each video capture session results in Movie Maker making a new collection and placing the thumbnail(s) for the clip(s) in it. In the case of an analog tape, there may be only one thumbnail for the entire file. With digital tapes, there will be multiple clips as determined by the timestamp on the tape.

Create a new collection (mine is called Chapter H2—Saugatuck) to contain the items needed for this project. I make subcollections for still pictures and video clips.

Move the three new video file icons from the collections created by Movie Maker (Summer 2002-1, 2, and 3) to the three new subcollections you made (Video 1, 2, 3) under Chapter H2—Day at Saugatuck. Drag and drop them from one to the other.

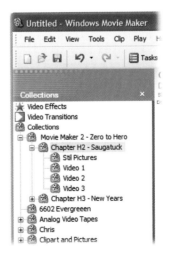

Moving source files

In addition to rearranging the collection tree and the contents of the collections, you may want to move or rename the video files on your computer so they are together in a folder for the project and on a drive that has sufficient space and has been recently defragmented. Because they were created in different folders during the capturing process, I moved the three DV-AVI files into a new folder for the project. The three files are 8.6GB, 1.4GB, and 5.1GB, for a total of 15.1GB. You need to close Movie Maker before moving these source files.

After moving them, restart Movie Maker and relink the thumbnails in your collections to the files that were moved or renamed. These thumbnails will have a big red X on them. Right-click one and choose Browse for Missing File… . Point Movie Maker to the file, and it'll re-establish the connection.

Reviewing the video and making clips

Video files created by Movie Maker from analog tapes (or digital tapes) may need you to create appropriate clips for the project. Select and copy the single big clip to make clips from the copy, leaving the original intact in case you need it. You can use the Ctrl+C and Ctrl+V keyboard shortcuts.

Make individual clips by playing the larger clip, finding the transition point between scenes by using the Next Frame and Previous Frame controls to find the points at which to split. Most often these will be the point at which one scene shot gives way to another.

Go to the first frame after the transition point between scenes and then use the Split button at the lower right of the monitor to do the splitting. The clip will be split into two, one for the footage before the split point and the other for the footage after it.

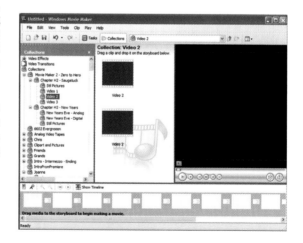

Give each new clip a new name, a sequential number for now. Sequential numbers will help when you are editing the timeline later, an easy way to know which sequence the scenes were taken in.

Importing still pictures

Any still pictures that you intend to use will have to be stored somewhere on your computer, having been captured from your digital camera (or scanner) already.

Select the collection folder for the project's still pictures, then select File > Import into Collections.... Choose those you want and Movie Maker adds the thumbnails for still pictures to the collection that you have selected.

Importing background music

There are many music selections already in my music collections in Movie Maker. I had selected tracks of a Fresh Aire VI album by Mannheim Steamroller to use as the background music.

When selecting the music tracks, it's a good time to use the option of looking at clip details instead of thumbnails. Music file thumbnails are all the same and provide no additional information. Right-click the thumbnails area and choose Arrange Icons By > Duration to make it easier to select potential pieces to fit into the planned timeframe—15 minutes for this project. Listen to each selection and pick the ones that will work best for your movie.

I selected "Sunrise at Rhodes" for opening credits and some beach scenes (four minutes), "Nepenthe" for town scenes (five and a half minutes), "The Olympics" for the kids running around and playing in town (two and a half minutes), and "Night Festival at Rhodes" for evening beach fun (four minutes). That adds up to 16 minutes, about right for this project.

Copy the music clips and paste them into the main collection for the project. My music source files are in WMA format.

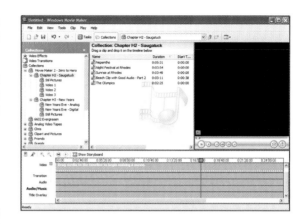

If you need to import music, as we did the still pictures, the music will be organized in the Movie Maker collection that you have highlighted when importing.

Creating the movie project

I almost always start a movie project with the background music if there is any, dragging a music clip onto the timeline.

Adding music

Toggle to the timeline view, as audio files can't go into the storyboard view, and drag the music files and drop them into the timeline Audio/Music track. The music sets the stage for adding the video and other visual pieces by defining the timeframe for each of the major segments. With a lot of clips to select from, it should be an appropriate way to define the project segments and start selecting clips for it.

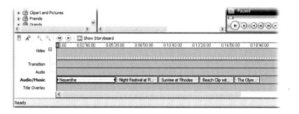

With the music on the timeline, consider your project as started. Name and save it (File > Save Project As), and get into the habit of saving it often. You can leave the project file in the default folder for project files or save it anywhere else on the computer.

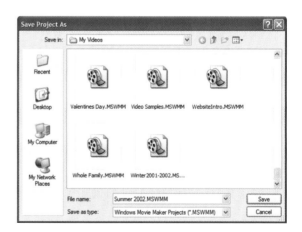

Project file names end with .MSWMM. The project file is not yet a movie file—you will create the movie file later from the project file.

Adding video clips and still pictures

Review the clips for the project. You may want to rename clips with numbers to more descriptive names. This is a personal preference—if it helps you, change them!

Change back to the storyboard view to start adding some video clips. I started with a pure black still picture that I had created.

Movie Maker has a fade-in/fade-out effect that replaces the need for continued use of a pure black still image. However, you may occasionally want to use another still picture or color to fade into and out of, and you can do this simply by replacing the black still with another still.

Select the opening clip, toggle to the timeline view, and drag it to about two seconds to the left to overlap the black picture. This will add a two-second fade-in from black to start the movie. Save the project, and save often, especially after each new step. Preview the timeline, watch the opening seconds, and listen to the start of the music.

Trimming the audio

The music on my audio track doesn't start for a while, and when it does start, it sounds like a horse trotting for a few seconds. I needed to clip some of audio track so the music would start when we want it to and with the music segments we want to align with the video in our project.

I split the audio to delete the dead time at the beginning and remove the sound of the trotting horse at the start. I selected the Audio/Music track, split the clip at the appropriate point using the Split icon under the Preview window, deleted the first part, and moved the second part to the left. It starts a few seconds after the beginning of the timeline. I watched it again and saw how much better the movie was already.

Adjusting audio levels

Add a second clip, then preview and check how the audio sounds. You may need to adjust or mute the audio on the early clips. I mute all except the clip with the lapping waves and adjust the audio for that one. Right-click on a clip and choose Volume to adjust the audio level for it.

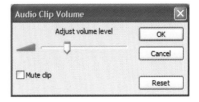

Filling the timeline

Work on filling in the storyboard/timeline with clips, remembering to save the project often. Work on aligning video clips with the music, muting and adjusting the volume of each clip as appropriate. Use black transition images between major segments of the video and leave text, special video effects, and complex transitions until the timeline is pretty well fleshed out.

Adding video transitions

With lots of video clips in the project, it's time to start adding some transitions. Select the Video Transitions collection and the thumbnail view of its contents. Select any of them; double-click to preview the transition effect in the monitor. To add a transition, use the storyboard view and drag the icon from the collection to the smaller box between the two clips.

To change a transition already on the storyboard, drag a different one to the transition box between the clips. The new one will replace the previous one. To delete a transition, select the transition box in the storyboard view and press the DELETE key.

When adding a transition, Movie Maker uses a default length of 1.25 seconds. If I want to make a transition longer, I toggle to the timeline view, grab the second clip of the two in the timeline, and drag it to the left to increase the amount of overlap between the two clips. This will automatically lengthen the time of the transition. To make one shorter, I drag the second clip to the right.

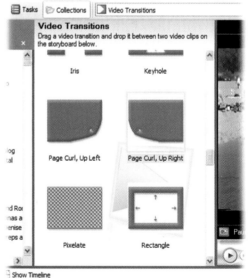

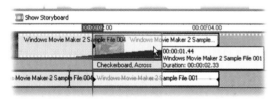

Extending a transition

Be careful how you use transitions; they really can alter the mood of a piece. The more obviously computer-generated tiles, fanning, bow ties, and stars, for example, do tend to look out of place in a more restfully paced movie. A modern transition may provide an unwelcome jump into the twenty-first century from old Super 8 footage! Unless that's what you intend, of course. I mostly used subtle fades in this movie.

Adding video effects

After transitions are in place, it's time to review the entire movie and perhaps incorporate a couple of effects. Be careful not to go overboard with effects. The novelty of them can wear off pretty quickly, so use only those that really add value to your movie.

You want people to be looking at and enjoying the video and pictures that you have, not marveling over the effects that the computer can do. Once seen, computer effects get old pretty quickly and your audience will then expect new effects with every new clip or movie.

Select one of the effects—let's preview the Rotate 180 effect. When the effect is selected from the list, the monitor will preview the effect, using the sample pictures provided with Movie Maker (or your own substituted ones—as shown here). Apply the effect to the clip by dragging it from the collection and dropping it on the selected clip.

As part of the final review of a movie, I'll consider adding an effect to a clip to help the overall flow of the movie. But I'll opt to replace poor clips with better ones, rather than use an effect to make a "wow!" statement. Focus on the quality of the content rather than special effects. Use them only when they really add value.

In the movie, I used effects on four of the 105 clips. The Fade Out, To Black and Fade In, From Black effects are perhaps more transitions than effects, but Movie Maker includes them in the set of effects.

Fading to and from black helps the viewer tell that a significant change in location or time has occurred. I used it in the movie when changing locations a couple times and on the very last clip to help smoothly end the movie.

The first use was to change from the scenes of my wife, Bernadette, walking along a path in the woods to an abrupt overview of the town from the top of a sand dune—a major change of location. I used the Fade Out, To Black on the last of three clips of her walking, followed by a Fade In, From Black on the town overview clip.

Then, at the end of overview clip of the town, I used the Fade Out, To Black again, followed by a Fade In, From Black on the following chain ferry clip. Again, I used this fade to accentuate the change in location from the top of the sand dune overlooking the town to being in the town itself.

One last Fade Out, To Black was used for the "PapaJohn Productions" still picture, the last clip in the movie.

Adding title text and credits

It's time to add lead-in text. Select the first clip (in my project, the black still picture) on the timeline, and from the menu, choose Tools > Titles and Credits.

Select Add title on the selected clip in the timeline and enter your text. I chose "Summer Holidays" on the first line and "July 2002" on the second, using the default font and alignment. When you're finished, select Done, add title to movie, and it'll appear on the timeline in the Title Overlay track.

On the second clip, I added another text title overlay that says "Saugatuck, Michigan," dragging the right edge of the newly added title to the right so that it overlaps with the next clip to some degree.

I added another title overlay, "Bernadette," this time changing the text Transparency to 26 percent so it's somewhat "see-through" and placed it under the clip Bernadette. The following clips showed each person on the trip, introducing the "cast," as it were. I then chose other title overlays for each person, using the same 26 percent transparency but with an appropriate alignment to match with the location of the person in the picture.

Adjust them as you want to align with the positions of the associated clips:

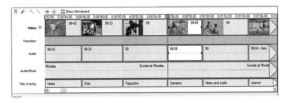

One reason for setting your video and audio clips before you do the titles is that if you move the clips on the timeline later during your editing, the title text overlay clips do not automatically move with their associated clips.

The impact of the text, especially as part of the opening segment of the movie, can increase the viewers' immediate positive feelings about your movie. Spend some time to make the opening as good as you can. The positive vibes from it will carry through and enhance the footage.

Adding closing credits

Closing credits are the last thing your audience sees of your movie, if they've made it that far, so it's another area worth spending that bit of extra effort on. I like to create the credits separately and then move them, positioning them as I want over other clips.

Select your ending clips and, from the drop-down menu, select Tools > Titles and Credits... and opt to Add credits at the end of the movie. Movie Maker adds scrolling credits to the end of the Video track, and I drag them down to the Title Overlay track and to the left, so some will play as an overlay on the final video clip(s).

I double-click the overlay to make changes to the effects, using the Fade, In and Out instead of the scrolling credits.

Finally I added a Newspaper title animation at the very end, the most unusual of the various text overlay effects.

A final review

When you have all your video, still images, music, transitions, and effects in place, it is time to review the entire movie with a critical eye. When you are personally satisfied with it, you might invite a few others to review it and make comments. Use their feedback to further fine-tune the movie before saving the final one. This is especially important if you plan to burn many CDs or DVDs to distribute your movie.

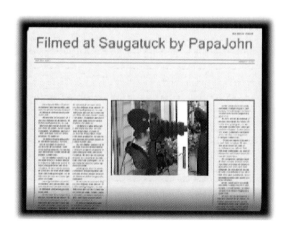

Audio tricks

Some of the video was taken with lots of wind noise affecting the microphone, and some of it had nice surf sounds without wind noise. I wanted to use a good audio segment from part of the footage while using the video from different footage, without affecting the music background. This isn't something that's easily done in Movie Maker (nor other video editing software that costs less than $300), due to there being only one Audio/Music track, but here's an approach.

Open a new project, and add the music track to it. Then select the clip with the good audio from your collections and drop it onto the timeline. Put additional copies of the video clip until it covers the full length of the music track.

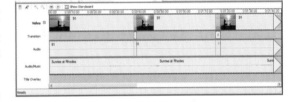

Save the movie with the good audio and music to your computer (File > Save Movie File... or CTRL+P) with the best file quality possible.

We can now open our main project again and import the file into our Collection folder (File > Import into Collections... or CTRL+I).

The new WMA file was 3 minutes and 49.26 seconds long, while the music file previously had been clipped at the beginning to be 3 minutes and 11.20 seconds. (Remember the horse noises?) So we need to split the new file at the 00:38:06 point to match the first music file, and then use the second part of the clipped file.

The thumbnail for the new clip shows video, but when you drag it to the timeline onto the Audio/Music track, it behaves as audio. Delete the original music file that was first used on the timeline and drag the new clip on to the timeline to replace it. Right-click on the new clip on the timeline and select Fade In.

This is the same method you could use if you had a number of source video clips and you wanted to use a single audio track from one of the video files; for example, if you wanted to mix clips taken at multiple angles while using the audio track from only one.

Putting the movie on a DVD or VCD

DVDs are now the premier format for video distribution, and some computers are equipped with DVD drives capable of recording these discs, but most aren't. Luckily, a great deal of DVD players will play another format VCD—which anyone with a CD-R drive can produce.

A Video CD (VCD) uses movie files in MPEG-1 format; Super VCDs (SVCD) and DVDs use files in MPEG-2 format, and Movie Maker does not make these. Another software application is needed to convert the file from Movie Maker into an MPEG file. Another software application is needed to create a menu for the viewer on the VCD/DVD. Some can do the conversion and create the menu, but I use two different applications.

Saving a DV-AVI file in Movie Maker 2

In Movie Maker, the first step toward a VCD, SVCD, or DVD is to save the movie as a digital video AVI file (DV-AVI). If the movie is as large as this 15-minute project, it's a good idea to defrag your hard drives before doing the final save. A contiguous movie file on your hard drive may help make the CD or DVD burning process successful.

I named it "Day at Saugatuck" and saved it in my project working folder (File > Save Movie File…). The Save Movie wizard defaults to the Best quality for playback on my computer option—select Show more choices... and choose DV-AVI (NTSC) or DV-AVI (PAL) if you're in Europe.

Click Next to create the movie. You can see the space required to make the file and the available space on the drive and rendering time.

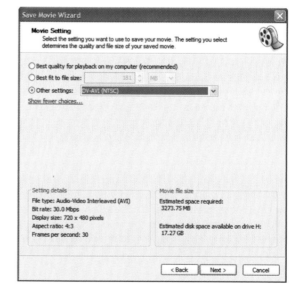

Rendering finished in 56 minutes, considerably less time than the original estimate. Movie Maker asks if you want to play the movie when finished. It's a good idea to watch it at this time, as it will be the version used to make your VCD, SVCD, or DVD. It will play in Windows Media Player.

The size of the saved movie file is 3.1GB, a size that might challenge some computer systems.

Making MPEG files with TMPGEnc

We'll use TMPGEnc, a very popular software application, to make both MPEG-1 and MPEG-2 files for our project. We will use the MPEG-1 file to burn a VCD.

TMPGEnc is available for download from www.tmpgenc.net. The freeware version encodes MPEG-1, whereas MPEG-2 encoding is limited to a 30-day trial. (The full version, TMPGEnc Plus, is $48.)

The first window of TMPGEnc asks you to select an MPEG file format. Select Video-CD, NTSC (or PAL in Europe) and go to the Next window.

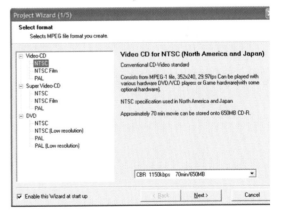

Select the video source file to convert, which is the DV-AVI file we saved from Movie Maker. It automatically fills in the Audio File field with the same file name. Leave the default settings and click Next.

The Filter setting window provides some options for fixing video files and some more advanced options. Leave the settings as they are and click Next.

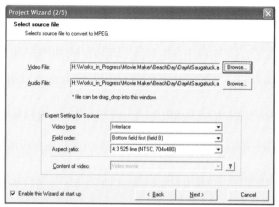

The Bit Rate Settings window gives you options to set the bit rate of the MPEG file you create. Leave the defaults, which show that you will be using 20 percent of the CD. Click Next.

Then you specify the location and file name for the new MPEG file. It assumes that you want the MPEG file in the same folder as the source DV-AVI file.

TMPGEnc then creates the MPEG file. When you first click OK, it tells you that the output file doesn't exist. Click OK at that message, and it'll start the conversion process. The DV-AVI file used as the input will remain and a new file will be created.

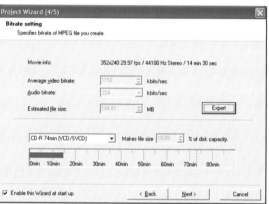

TMPGEnc shows you a preview of the movie as it is being created. My movie took about 50 minutes to be converted and MPEG-1 file was 151MB, about five percent of the size of the input DV-AVI file. You can use the same process with TMPGEnc to create an MPEG-2 file for a SVCD or DVD, a number of preset options are available—accessed by the Load button, at the bottom right of the main window.

Creating a VCD with menu

By using specialized software for making the menu and burning a CD or DVD, you can place a number of 15-minute movies on a VCD, SVCD, or DVD. Here I'll mention some of the popular software choices, but I use ULead's DVD Workshop to create a menu for my project and burn a VCD that will play in a DVD player.

Roxio Easy CD Creator is available for download from www.roxio.com. You may already have the basic software, having received it with the CD-RW drive of your computer. Insert a blank CD in your CD-RW drive and select Create a CD using Roxio from the choices in the window that opens. Note that the option to create a VCD will be unavailable unless you upgrade to Easy CD Creator 5 Platinum.

Nero is a very popular choice to burn CDs and DVDs. It is available for download from www.nero.com and provides a free 30-day trial period. Many people love this software and the 30-day trial period should help you assess it close up for your needs.

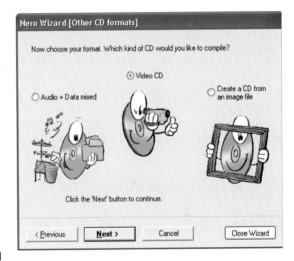

Using Ulead DVD Workshop

ULead's DVD Workshop can create VCDs, SVCDs, and DVDs, and we will use it to burn a VCD to finish this project. A trial version is available from www.ulead.com/dws/.

Open DVD Workshop and create and name a new project.

Load our MPEG-1 project file into the library that we had created with TMPGEnc and preview it.

Select Menu from the bar at the top of the screen and a menu template style from the wizard.

Click Finish and you can then edit the information, text styles, background picture, and buttons as you see fit.

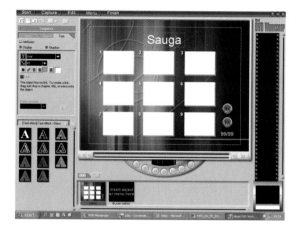

When you're happy with your menu and you have all the movie clips you'd like in the project, you have created your VCD. In our case, there's only one movie to be put onto the disc, although you could fit more if you had them.

Click Finish (in the bar at the top) to create the VCD. ULead DVD Workshop will then burn your disc.

Test the CD by playing it on your computer, on a couple of other computers if you have them available, and then on a DVD player.

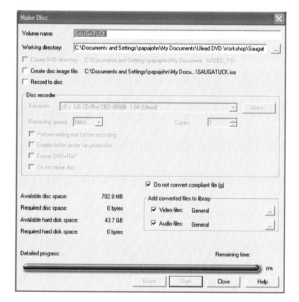

Using Movie Maker 2 to burn a CD

Movie Maker has an option to save the movie directly to a recordable CD by using the recently announced HighMAT format (see **Chapter 9**). The rendering process takes as much CPU power as the computer can spare, taking all your source files as defined in the project spec and making a playable movie file.

The rendering process saves the movie in a temporary file and then copies it to a recordable CD, offering you the option of making more than one CD from the temporary file.

When the process is completed, Movie Maker gives you the option of making another CD. Because the rendering of the project has already been completed to make the temporary file, the second, third, etc. CDs are created pretty quickly, about the same it takes to copy a CD.

The HighMAT format is similar quality to a VCD, SVCD, or DVD. The CD that is created will play on any computer running Windows Media Player 7 or later. The file for this 15-minute movie is only 173MB.

When you insert the CD in a computer, it should start automatically and play in Windows Media Player (WMP). Computers running Windows 98, ME, 2000, and XP should have no difficulty running it. If the computer is connected to the Internet, WMP will automatically obtain any extra software from the Microsoft server and will play the movie smoothly.

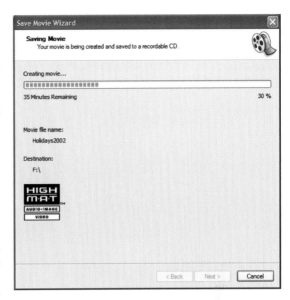

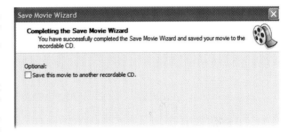

You're ready for the premiere!

Enjoy the process as you go. You, your family, and friends will love the movies that you make. Movie Maker is all you need to start the process rolling.

Producing a short movie for the web

Jen deHaan

In this chapter

Producing any video involves a lot of planning, scripting, storyboarding, and shooting, as well as editing. But if you are going to put the finished video on the Internet, you must consider the message and the medium as one. Throughout your preproduction, production, and postproduction processes, you will need to consider not just what you are shooting and editing, but how.

The aim for this particular production is to tell a story through imagery, text, and sound. There will be no dialog or narration; we'll focus on the imagery of a city in the depths of winter. We'll also discuss compression, a great and complex subject on its own. So, we'll cover the following:

★ Writing and working from a script
★ Shooting on location, lighting and sound
★ Preproduction for the movie
★ Editing the video
★ Video for the web
★ ISPs and bandwidth
★ Streaming and progressive download
★ Outputting for the web
★ Encoding by using Windows Media Encoder
★ Putting your files online
★ Understanding the target audience
★ HTML pages
★ Using Flash MX for WMV presentation

Organizing and working with a script

As always, thorough preproduction will save you a lot of time and effort in the long run. Working with a script is quite different from working with storyboards. Scripts are written documents that describe the locations and events of a movie and also contain all the dialog spoken by the characters. Storyboards, on the other hand, are a pictorial series that depict the events in the movie.

You can choose to work with one of these or even both. Some people work better with one in particular, but using both a script and a storyboard can give you even more of a plan and a better idea of how to implement them. At the very least, it's a good idea to make a few storyboard sketches of the major scenes in your script. It's beneficial to sketch any difficult or complex shots and have them on hand when you are in filming process. This will help you a great deal when you are shooting the video.

Typical aspects of a script

There is a fine art to scriptwriting, and there are conventions that are practiced throughout the movie-making industry. Although these go beyond what you need to do when working alone, you should consider the conventions when preparing a script a they really will help.

- ★ **Consider the genre of your script**. Is it horror, a love story, drama, documentary, or comedy? There are many predetermined genres, so where does your script fall?
- ★ **Write a short description of the plot**. Think about any foreshadowing or flashbacks as well, and note if and when they're applicable.
- ★ **List the characters**. What are their names, physical attributes, and demeanors? What are the characters like? What are their most prominent traits and what are their personalities like?
- ★ **Write dialog**. What do the characters say? You might also include where the dialog is coming from. Is it a voice over (VO), or does it come from off screen (OS)?

★ **Divide the script into scenes**. This will help you organize the script.

★ **Describe the scenes and locations**. Use descriptive words and include whether they are interior (INT) or exterior (EXT) shots.

Breaking down your script

After you have developed a script for your movie, break that script down into sections. These might be either scenes or "parts" of your video and might typically be the different locations where you are shooting your footage.

For this video, the footage was shot at only three different locations but has six different "scenes." Therefore, in preproduction, the video was broken into three different parts for organizational purposes: *the lake*, *the park*, and *home*, and this helped develop the scenes more clearly. Consider creating a very basic storyboard of the major scenes. This will definitely help you when you are on location.

If you are shooting people or particular subjects, you will need to consider what kind of shots you will need to gather. Think about such shots as

★ **Close-up shots**
★ **Medium shots**
★ **Long shots**
★ **Subjective shots**, which include
    ★ **Point-of-view shots**
    ★ **Over-the-shoulder shots** (as here)

The first three are pretty obvious and show differing amounts of detail and action. Point-of-view shots show what one character would see; over-the-shoulder shots show the action from a little behind a character. Directing and the specifics of filmmaking go well beyond what we can cover here, but if you've ever watched any TV or films, you'll probably find that most of it will be second nature.

Shooting on location

As opposed to shooting in the confines of your house, shooting on location can bring up a whole new set of challenges; you have many elements to think about and plan for. You might be working in an area with many people around or be filming while working with a small crew. Whatever your circumstances are, it is a good idea to think of all the different things that could potentially happen beforehand.

- ★ What if the weather changes during the shoot?
- ★ What if pedestrians become a problem?
- ★ Who is in front of and behind the camera?
- ★ Where do I need to go?
- ★ Who will perform each task, if you have a crew?
- ★ What if the lighting is poor?
- ★ What if I am asked to leave the location? Where do I go then?

These are only a few of the questions you might have about the shoot. Plan ahead, and make lists! It is a good idea to have back-up plans and help during any shoot that's on location. If you have a budget and perhaps have or are renting equipment, make sure that you have a place to plug in batteries, lights, and so on. Lighting, as discussed in the next section, is very important and can make or break your footage.

Be careful, and make sure that you get the proper permission (or read about the legal technicalities in your country) in advance.

Lighting for the movie

Whether you are shooting your footage indoors or outdoors, lighting should be a concern. If you do not have professional-style lighting for your shots, I advise that you try to make the area you are shooting in as light as possible or choose a day that's bright.

When indoors, try to light the environment as much as possible. You might want to try shining desk lamps on your subject, which can add definition and contrast. As you can see in part of the video made for this chapter, there is *not* enough light on the subjects.

As you can see here, even though there is one directional light casting some interesting shadows, it would have been beneficial to have a second light behind the camera shining on the black cat's face. Several directional lights will dramatically improve this kind of situation.

When using artificial lights, you must be aware of the color of the picture. Using desk lamps indoors will cast an orange light on your image. If your camera has a **white balance** function, you need to use it to tell the camera what sort of white is in your artificially lit room, then it can work out the rest of the colors. This will remove any color cast from the picture.

> *It is much easier to work with quality footage than to attempt to "fix" it by using software packages afterward. Movie Maker is not made for correcting color professionally, so take care to take the best footage you can!*

You might be surprised about light levels outdoors. In fact, overcast days have the best overall light levels and make for an ideal environment for shooting footage. That said, a sunny day can afford a great opportunity for creating dramatic highlights and shadows. If you can, choose days that best reflect what effect or mood that you need to achieve, and consider using a **reflector** (a piece reflective material, typically circular) to enhance the level of light on your subjects.

Audio: soundtracks and narrations

You probably have dialog, narrations (or voice-overs), or soundtracks planned for your video. You might even have a combination of all these elements! I strongly advise that you plan what you are going to do *before* you begin gathering your video footage. Obviously, when working from a script, you will need to prepare it well in advance.

For top-quality audio, either naturally occurring background noise or dialog, you will need to have a microphone handy, something more than what is built in to your camera. You have a few options, some of the more common being

- ★ Boom microphone (attached to a boom pole)
- ★ Shotgun microphone (highly directional microphone)

★ Lavaliere microphone (clip-on microphone)
★ Condenser or dynamic microphone

Microphones tend to vary greatly in price and quality, so it's wise to do some research before spending money on buying or renting equipment.

Because this video is using a soundtrack as opposed to dialog, we will not require the use of a microphone. There will not be any dialog or narration in this video, but it will instead focus on the imagery of a city in the depths of winter.

Computers and software

When you are making a movie, don't feel like you're restricted to one piece of software. Sometimes, it is easier or better to use different software packages along with Movie Maker to create elements for your production. Before starting production, take a minute to consider what you need to get the project done. Also, take an inventory of the resources available to you, from equipment to software packages.

We'll keep it simple here; titles and captions are easily added to any Movie Maker movie. But we already have some very simple Photoshop-made graphic stills, which we'll add to the production.

Many graphics are too complicated to create by using Movie Maker. Creating your own images in a separate graphic editing program will give you a lot more flexibility. We'll discuss this later on in the chapter.

Creating the audio

No narration is planned for the documentary being created for this chapter. This is a conscious decision, based on the premise to focus on the imagery of Toronto in the winter, as opposed to a vocal narration that would likely detract from that.

Adding some sound to the production is necessary and usually adds a lot more depth to any work. We are using Reason 2.0 to create the background music. Reason is an audio program made by Propellerheads, and it is typically used for loops, songs, and audio mixing/editing. It is a wonderful and fully featured piece of software. Obviously, using Reason is a very complex subject, but you can find out more information on it at the following web sites:

★ Download the demo and documentation at: www.propellerheads.se/replacehardware.

★ Tutorials and refills can be found at www.reasonstation.net.

★ Get more tutorials and download refills at www.reasonfreaks.com.

I'd encourage you to check out this software, as it is a lot of fun and very useful if you ever need to add audio to your productions or web sites.

Resources and inspiration

It's always wise to look at other videos in the same genre before starting production. Inspiration doesn't mean you have to copy other people's ideas; researching will help you generate different ones of your own.

It doesn't hurt to take a look and get some ideas, even if you're not sure how (or can't afford) to carry them out. Before starting production, I watched *Baraka* (1992, Fricke—you can see more about this and watch a trailer online at http://us.imdb.com/Title?0103767) as an example of a video that was not narrated but told a strong story by using only music and visuals.

Opening Movie Maker 2

Once you have gathered all your source footage, it is time to open Movie Maker and begin editing. As usual, I start by checking the program's settings.

Using title stills

In this project, we use stills that have been prepared by using Photoshop. They are very simple stills, consisting of white text on a black background, so they could be created in any simple image editing program in any font. The graphics were made the same dimensions as the video. We'll discuss how we use them later on in the chapter.

The font I've used in this chapter is called Nail Scratch and is available as freeware, which means that you can use it without paying any copyright fees. It, and other fonts, can be downloaded from www.misprintedtype.com.

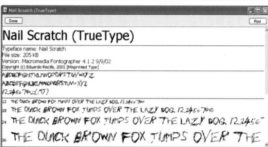

Because this video is being created for the web as opposed to the TV, you do not need to worry about title-safe or action-safe areas for the text or footage that you are using. If you think it might be viewed on a television, make sure that you place all your text well away from the edges of the viewing area.

We will be importing many of these pictures into the production. Before getting started, always check the settings under Tools > Options.

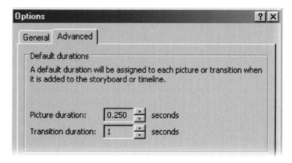

Each of these pictures will be visible for only a fraction of a second, in most cases. Therefore, you need to set the picture duration to only 0.25 seconds. Some pictures will need to have a longer duration, but this can be accomplished manually by using the trim handles in timeline view.

> While you're there, double-check your Temporary storage setting under the General tab, and make sure it is set to a drive with enough room for your video output.

Importing your source files and footage

Before you start editing, you have to import your video into Movie Maker. You should capture your video from your DV camera and import video clips, stills, graphics, and audio by using File > Import into Collections.

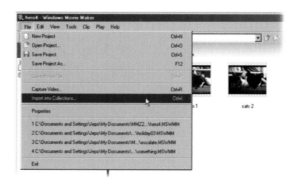

The video clips have been placed into several different collections, depending on the content, and I will probably divide them into different scenes. There are also many still images that need to be imported into each of these collections.

After importing the graphic stills, I have a mixture of stills and video clips in each collection. I did this to help organize the stills into their respective content areas. All the text on these stills is related to the video content in its collection.

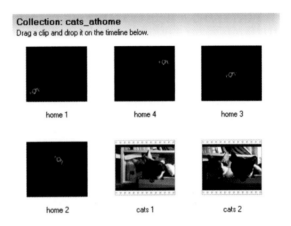

Collection: cats_athome
Drag a clip and drop it on the timeline below.

home 1   home 4   home 3

home 2   cats 1   cats 2

There is also some background music for this production. I imported it into a new collection. We'll go into more depth about the audio for this production soon.

Organizing your clips into collections

It is easier to work with a large piece of content when it is separated into smaller, contained areas. Your production will probably contain scenes, themes, or natural divisions. For a large project such as this, separate your content into these major divisions in the movie. For this movie, different locations were shot, and some of these areas had different themes. As you can see, each different location or theme is divided into its own collection.

Collections
Video Effects
Video Transitions
Collections
   cats_athome
   ice
   lake
   sky
   walk
   Windows Movie Maker 2 Sample File

Within each collection are several video clips that were captured earlier. You should import any stills directly related to the clips into each folder. This might include any photographic stills or graphics you have made in Photoshop.

Organization is of utmost importance in larger productions, particularly when you are working with stills and graphics. It is very easy to overlook or forget about content when it is poorly arranged in one large folder. You will probably want to make sure your file names are somewhat descriptive about your content as well. A video of your friend running away called "video 12" will be much less useful to you than something like "Scott running."

Collection: sky
Drag a clip and drop it on the timeline below.

sky 1   sky 2   sky 3

Stating to edit

After completing preproduction, there are things to think about as you start dragging your video clips onto the timeline. You need to consider how you're going to edit your work so that it looks good after it is heavily compressed to go on the web.

Adding clips while considering the output

Compressing video can alter the quality of your video significantly, but there are several things you can consider beforehand to help you take footage that will compress well. One of the main things that will not compress well is random, moving pixels and gradients (caused by rapid movement in the picture). If your footage has already been taken (as in this case), it is too late and you will simply have to deal with this during compression. We already have those situations (a sunset, snow, and wind) occurring in the footage.

Editing the footage can help, or hinder, the efforts you make during the compression process. Really long "cross-fades" (the Fade transition) do not compress well, usually resulting in blockiness. We have tried to work around this by using very short Fade transitions in the movie.

Adding titles and captions

As usual, a title animation has been added at the beginning of the video. A particular font has been used throughout this video. This font adds a certain feel to the video overall and has been chosen specifically because of this. It is always wise to carefully choose a font, whether you are working with graphics or editing video.

Instead of using Movie Maker to create captions within the video, original text-laden transitions have been created by importing stills. This is discussed in the next section.

Credits were added to the end of the video by using the Make titles or credits option in the tasks pane. We've maintained the same font and background color throughout the video for the sake of continuity. This is usually quite important when you want to create a professional feel in any production.

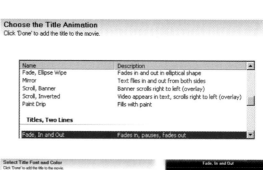

Adding transitions and effects to the video

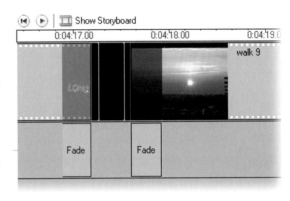

Movie Maker's transitions and effects have been used very sparingly in this video. However, some original "transitions" were used. For this video, a number of graphic "stills" were imported and used for transitional effects. These stills, as mentioned earlier, were created by using Adobe Photoshop 7 (although any image editor could be used for this purpose). They were placed between video clips and Fade transitions were used on both sides.

The text is intended to make additions to the meaning of the video. It will also help smooth the transitions in the footage because sometimes the changes are quite drastic.

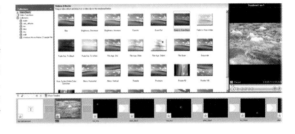

Because of the natural feel of this video, very few video effects have been used. The fade in and out to and from black did come in very useful, though, and both have been added to the beginning and end of the movie. Also, the Brightness, Increase effect has been used on a couple of clips that were too dark. This helped clarify the subjects being shot to some degree and also made the footage look higher quality.

Adding the audio

An audio track was created by using Propellerhead's Reason software, a tool that is commonly used for audio editing and creating loops. The 54-second piece (that was made to loop) has been imported into a new collection called audio and the clip is called background_music.

Luckily, it is a very easy process to add looping audio to a movie in this software. In timeline view, drag and drop the audio clip from the audio collection onto the Audio/Music track. You might want to line up the audio clip to the end of the movie's title at the beginning.

Collection: audio
Drag a clip and drop it on the timeline below.

background_music

Directly following this first audio loop, drag and drop a second loop onto the Audio/Music track. If you pull the audio clip toward the one placed before it, it'll snap into place directly after that clip, creating a seamless loop.

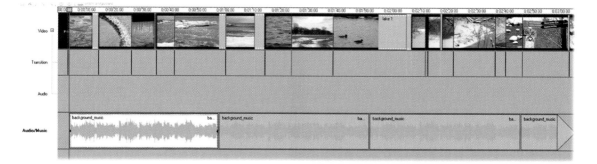

Continue in this manner until you have reached the end of your movie.

Because we have created an audio piece that loops, it doesn't necessarily match with the end of the movie that was edited. Therefore, we need to trim it to match the end of the final video clip (which is the end credits). Select the audio clip and use the trim handles to trim it to the same length as the video content.

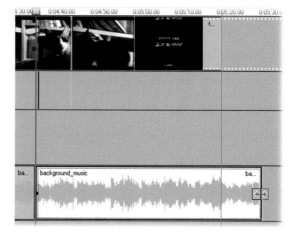

You can also fade in and fade out the audio or music in your movie. We're going to fade out the soundtrack at the end of the movie. Right-click on the audio clip and choose Fade Out from the context menu.

Once finishing the audio track, you are done! The final step in the editing process is to check the video for anything that might have been overlooked.

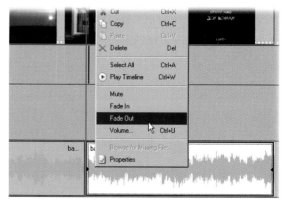

Refining the video

By now, you have probably made a few videos and will realize the importance of testing the rendering process. Render a few low-quality videos to check if there are any glitches in the video or if you have missed any desired effects or transitions. It will also give you a good enough idea about how your video is before you create a final copy.

Even if you plan to create a copy only for the web, you might also want to create a good-quality version for archival purposes. If file size on your hard drive is a concern, then consider transferring a copy to DV tape.

Outputting video for the web

Putting video online can be more complicated than it initially seems. There are many different areas to consider when putting such content online. You have to be aware of what video players, codecs, bandwidth, and connection speeds the end user has if you plan to target a wide audience.

ISP allowances

Not every ISP's (Internet Service Provider) server will allow streaming video content, and ones that do will have certain formats that you can use on the server depending on what software they have installed. You can either stream your WMV files by using a special streaming server or have them progressively downloaded from a regular web server.

Streaming and downloading files

A streaming server can be used to "broadcast" premade video files such as those made by using Movie Maker. Your video downloads a certain amount of content, called **buffering**, and then begins streaming to the end user. The advantage of this is that the end user does not need a very fast connection to enjoy video content that is streamed, allowing you to reach a wider audience.

Just as there are different kinds of file formats, there are different kinds of streaming web server software. Real, QuickTime, Windows Media, and even Macromedia Flash have their own streaming server software. You'll have to find a hosting provider that is compatible with the way you prepare your video files. The providers linked to by Movie Maker (when you choose the Send to the Web option) work with WMV files, or you can find your own.

You don't need to stream your video files; you can upload the files to any web server and then embed them in a web page. These WMV files will be downloaded to the end user and can be played once they've been loaded. Windows Media Player can emulate the buffering effect of streaming by starting to play the video before it's all arrived, but there is no need for a dedicated server.

Monitoring your bandwidth

Regardless of the way you offer your video files, you will also have to be careful about your **bandwidth**. This is the amount of data that is transferred when someone downloads or streams your movie when looking at it on a web page. In most cases, you will have a certain amount of bandwidth allocated to your account. Once you reach that limit, you will probably have to pay extra money to your hosting provider. Therefore, it is advised that you closely watch how much bandwidth you use. If you are only showing a short, compressed video to a small number of people, you won't need to worry about bandwidth.

Encoding the video with Movie Maker 2

As usual, you use the Save Movie wizard to create your finished movie. Movie Maker will compress and save the file and then automatically try to upload it to a recommended service provider. If you want to upload the movie to your own web space, you can disconnect your Internet connection and still use the Send to the Web option. You can do this by removing the cable or just by clicking Cancel when the dial-up process starts.

1. Select the option to Send to the Web from the tasks pane, or open the wizard and select the web option.

2. Give your video a file name and then select the video setting that will be best for your target audience.

If you know exactly the type of Internet connection that your audience has, you can select the nearest from the Other settings drop-down box. If you're not sure, you have to make a guess based on who you think the audience might be and decide on the Video Settings accordingly.

After the movie has rendered, you will see a dialog box similar to the one here. If there are any, under Provider name:, you will see the names of a number of video hosting providers in a drop-down box that are local to your area.

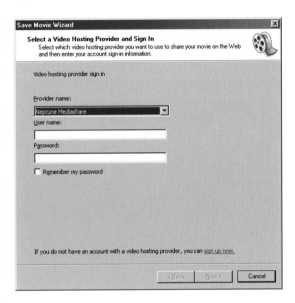

3. If you want to use one of these services, you will have to sign up to get a user name and password. Sign in and Movie Maker will automatically upload your movie to the web.

4. If there are no providers in your area or your computer is not connected to the Internet, you will be offered the opportunity to save the movie to your computer. Save it and upload your video to your own hosting provider at any time. If you play your video, you can check out the quality of compression.

Movie Maker's implementation of saving for the web is not very useful for those of us not using one of the selected hosting providers, and we hope that this will be better implemented in a future version of the program.

Understanding the end user

It is important to think about who is going to view your movie, and this should give you some direction in deciding how to present your work online. You will need to think about the most common speed of Internet connection the end user will have, what kind of plug-ins and codecs are installed, the browser and platform, and so on. This section will help you understand different kinds of computer setups and help you to create movies directly targeted at the people who you'd like to watch them.

Your audience and Internet connections

If most of your end users are on a phone modem and your WMV file is 40MB, then most of these people will give up long before they download the movie. It will simply take way too long to see the content. However, if you have trimmed and compressed the movie down to 6MB, then these users will probably wait for it to download and play.

So what affects file size? All sorts of things: the size of your frames (the movie dimensions), frame rate, data rate, and even how much movement is in your video! With downloadable WMV files, if you have a lot of solid areas, your movie file will be smaller than one with lots of pixel movement. Branches blowing in the wind will make for a bigger video file than a person sitting still and talking.

If you are planning on showing your video to many different people online, try to have a couple of different versions of your movie available. You will want to make a larger one for people with fast connections and a smaller one for those with a slow connection.

Browser plug-ins

If you have spent much time online, you have probably either heard of or installed different video players (as plug-ins for your browser). But because there are so many different ones out there, it stands to reason that not all users will have the same video player plug-ins.

The problem with the WMV format is that it is not compatible with all plug-ins, only Windows Media Player. If you know that some of your audience will not have Windows Media Player installed, you will have to use other software to produce additional files.

If you save your movie as an AVI file (see **Chapter 9**), you could open your video by using QuickTime Pro and then save your movie in the MOV format. Or, you could use any number of compression software packages (such as Cleaner from www.discreet.com) to compress your movie.

Codecs

Whatever codec you are using to create your movie will be needed by the end user to play it on their end. Windows Media Player will attempt to download the codec automatically when the user plays the movie, and this will work if you are using Movie Maker or the Microsoft Encoder to encode your movies.

However, if you do run into problems with people not being able to play your movie (and they do have the browser plug-in), then not having the proper codec might be the problem.

Putting your movie on a web page

There are several different ways that you can put your movie on the web, in addition to using Movie Maker's built-in features. This section will show you how to put your movie online manually on a HTML web site. Knowing how to do this will enable you to customize your web site for a wider audience, offering more than one version in the same place.

Embedding the movie in an HTML page

Microsoft's recommended way to put a WMV file online only allows an Internet Explorer-based audience to view your content. Doing it this way will enable your audience to use either Internet Explorer or Netscape (or Mozilla!) to view your content.

Unless you are absolutely certain the people who will view your movie are using Internet Explorer on a PC, it is a good idea to use this method.

1. The first step is to create a Windows **meta file** that contains a reference to your video. We will assume for this example that the video's name is `myVideo.wmv`. Also remember to replace the `http://yourserver` with the address of your own web server in these files.

2. In Notepad (or whatever editor you use for creating web pages), type the following code:

```
<ASX version = "3.0">
<Entry>
<Ref
href="http://yourserver/myVideo.wmv"
/>
</Entry>
</ASX>
```

> If you are streaming your video from a streaming server, you would instead use the following address: `mms://yourserver/myVideo.wmv`

3. Save this file as `myVideo.wvx`. Although you don't absolutely need a meta file, it is a practice recommended by Microsoft.

4. Now type the following code into a new HTML web page and save it as `myvideo.html`:

```
<html>
<head>
<title>Link to a video</title>
</head>
<body>
Click <a href="http://yourserver/
➥myVideo.wvx">here</a> for my video.
</body>
</html>
```

5. Upload both of these files and your WMV video file to your web space (your ISP will tell you exactly how).

Within the myvideo.html web page, the preceding code will appear as a simple link. When a person clicks on the word here, it will either play the file in Internet Explorer or open the video in Windows Media Player.

> Remember that your end user will have to have the Windows Media Player installed on their system, which will work in both Netscape and Internet Explorer.

Embedding the movie in a browser window

If you'd like to see a more advanced way of doing this, please check out my web site. You can copy and paste all the source code I mention in this chapter, as well as this advanced method: www.flash-mx.com/moviemaker2.

If you are interested in building your own web sites, then you will need more information than this book can supply. There are many good online resources — but if you would like to use a book, then www.friendsofed.com is a good place to start looking.

Take a look

For a finished version of the video that was made for this chapter, go to the friends of ED web site and look up *Movie Maker 2 Zero to Hero*. The video is available for download and is approximately 6MB large.

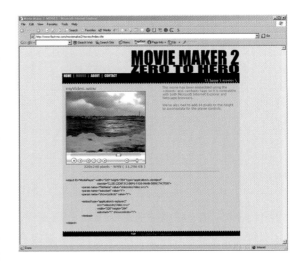

Index

The index is arranged hierarchically in alphabetical order. Many second-level entries also occur as first-level entries. This is to ensure that you will find the information you require however you choose to search for it.

friends of ED particularly welcomes feedback on the layout and structure of this index. If you have any comments or criticisms, please visit www.friendsofed.com.

W

Z